SAINT *of* PHILADELPHIA

Saint John Neumann
[Original sketch by Brother Robert Martin, C.SS.R.]

SAINT *of* PHILADELPHIA

The Life of
Bishop John Neumann

(1811 - 1860)

PHILIP DOUGLAS

THE RAVENGATE PRESS
Cambridge

1991 Edition

Nihil obstat:
REV. FRANCIS D. KELLY
Censor Deputatus

Imprimatur:
+BERNARD J. FLANAGAN
Bishop of Worcester
June 10, 1977

The *Nihil obstat* and *Imprimatur* are official declarations that a book or pamphlet is free of doctrinal and moral error. No implication is contained therein that those who have granted the *Nihil obstat* and *Imprimatur* agree with the content, opinions or statements expressed.

Please address orders and inquiries to:
The Ravengate Press
Post Offfice Box 49
Still River, Massachusetts 01467

ISBN: 0-911218-07-6   (Clothbound)
ISBN: 0-911218-08-4   (Paperbound)

Foreword

NO ONE WHO ATTEMPTS A SERIOUS STUDY of Saint John Neumann can afford to ignore the two standard and scholarly accounts of his life: *Life of the Right Reverend John N. Neumann, Fourth Bishop of Philadelphia*, by his nephew, Rev. John N. Berger, C.SS.R., published in German in 1883 and translated a year later into English, and *Bishop John Neumann, C.SS.R., Fourth Bishop of Philadelphia*, by the late Rev. Michael J. Curley, C.SS.R., now published by the Bishop Neumann Center in Philadelphia. I am especially grateful to Father Francis J. Litz, C.SS.R., Vice-Postulator of the cause of St. John Neumann and Director of the Bishop Neumann Center, for permission to use material from Father Curley's book, and for lending me his own personal copy of Father Berger's work. Father Litz also provided many of the pictures which appear in these pages, and supplied several unpublished anecdotes from the life of St. John Neumann. Thanks are also due to Brother Barnabas D. Hipkins, C.SS.R., Archivist of the Redemptorist Provincial Archives in Brooklyn, for additional pictures and aid.

I would like to insert here a brief explanation about terminology. The Congregation of the Most Holy Redeemer, the religious community to which St. John

Neumann belonged, is not, strictly speaking, a religious *order*, but is rather what its name says it is: a *congregation*. There are important differences in Church Law between the two, but at the risk of offending more knowledgeable readers, I have used both *order* and *congregation* in referring to the Redemptorists. This certainly reflects the more popular practice, and is one which I feel will be more understandable to a majority of readers.

Saint John Neumann is the third American citizen to be canonized, the second within two years, but there are also other candidates under consideration. Some were born in this country; some were not, but they all labored and sacrificed to establish the Church in America and to bring it to maturity. They have left us an example of courage and dedication—and an obligation to carry on the work they began.

P. D.

Contents

Illustrations

ILLUSTRATIONS [Continued]

Bishop Neumann's home, Logan Square, Philadelphia

1

The Fifth of January

PHILADELPHIA, January 5, 1860. Over the hopes and expectations which every New Year brings, there were this year clouds of worry and foreboding. The bitter division of the country over the issue of slavery could scarcely be contained much longer, and thinking men were already wondering how this election year of 1860 would end.

Only the previous October a zealous abolitionist named John Brown had led a party of men in seizing the United States Arsenal at Harpers Ferry, Virginia, his declared purpose being to organize and arm the slaves to fight for their freedom. U. S. Marines under the temporary command of Army Colonel Robert E. Lee made short work of the rebellion, but several men were killed in the exchange, and Brown was tried and convicted of treason. He was hanged on December second, and his hopeless gamble seemed over, but the abolitionists had a martyr, and the country was not permitted to forget John Brown. By December of the New Year, 1860, South Carolina had seceded from the Union, and four months later another United States Government installation, Fort Sumter in Charleston harbor, was captured, this time by the Confederates. When Sumter was fired upon, there was no turning back, and the greatest, most terrible war ever fought in our hemisphere began its savage course.

Concern and worry over what the New Year would bring cannot have been far from the mind of the short man in black who left his home in Philadelphia's Logan Square on that Thursday afternoon, the fifth of January, 1860, to do a few important errands. He was after all the bishop of this city, and he knew that if war did come, many of his people would suffer and die.

And yet, war, slavery and the troubles facing his adopted country may not on that day have been foremost in the mind of the Most Reverend John Nepomucene Neumann, fourth Bishop of Philadelphia. He had not been feeling well, and perhaps he had a premonition of what was about to happen. He had remarked to a visiting priest, "I have a strange feeling today. I feel as I never felt before," and a few moments later, "A man must always be ready, for death comes when and where God wills it." Before the day was over, these words would become terribly significant.

Almost certainly it would have been better for

Saint John Neumann
[Original photograph taken in 1852]

Bishop Neumann if he had not gone out feeling as he did, but there were things he had promised to do. A priest in a mountain parish had sent a new chalice to be consecrated by the Bishop, and the express company had somehow misplaced it. Bishop Neumann had written the priest that he would try to trace the package. A lawyer was waiting with some papers to be signed—important papers about property transfers— property for the Church to expand as the city of Philadelphia grew and expanded, property for new churches, charitable institutions and schools—schools above all. Bishop Neumann's great ambition was to provide Catholic schools for the people of his diocese, good schools staffed by competent and dedicated teachers who would instill into the young minds in their charge not only the three *R's* and a love and appreciation of their country and its history, but also a knowledge of and devotion to their "pearl of great price," their Catholic Faith.

The bishop had finished his business with the lawyer and was walking back in the direction of his home. All his life he had walked, had in fact preferred it to riding whenever he could. He walked west on Vine Street until he reached Thirteenth. As he crossed to the opposite side, he was seized with a sudden spasm. He staggered forward a few steps and then collapsed on the sidewalk. Two men who were passing rushed to his assistance and carried him, half unconscious, up the steps of the nearest house. They laid the bishop on the floor in front of the fire. He was recognized from his pectoral cross as Bishop

THE FIFTH OF JANUARY

Neumann, and someone rushed off to the Cathedral
to summon a priest, but it was too late. There on the
floor of a stranger's house, without the Last
Sacraments or any of the consolations the Church has
ready for her children in their last moments, the
Shepherd of the Church in Philadelphia rendered up
his soul to appear before the throne of God and give
an account of his stewardship. He was about three
months short of his forty-ninth birthday.

"What would you do," someone once asked St.
John Berchmans, the young Jesuit novice, "if you
knew you would die today?"

"I would continue doing what I am doing now,"
was his reply.

It happened to be community recreation time, and
John Berchmans was playing billiards. He could
answer as he did because he knew it was his duty to
be at recreation, and he was ready at any time to
appear before his Lord. "Watch therefore, because
you know not the day nor the hour."

John Neumann was ready too. Whether he had any
advance knowledge of what was about to happen, or
how he commended himself to God as he felt the
attack coming on, we do not know, but he spent his
last hours, as he had spent most of his life, in the
service of God and of the flock given to his care. The
Church has proclaimed his virtues heroic, and has
declared him a saint, the third American citizen to be
canonized, and the first man.

His life was not spectacular in any way. To many
of his contemporaries he did not appear to be any

different from any other priest or bishop, but in reality he was different—he was one of God's saints, given to us for our inspiration and imitation. In the pages that follow we shall try to unfold his story, from his birth in Bohemia to his death on that wintry day in Philadelphia.

2

Bohemian Background

SURROUNDED BY A CIRCLE OF MOUNTAINS, Bohemia sits comfortably in the middle of Middle Europe. The name is probably of Celtic origin, and commemorates the first recorded settlers, but some time between the first and fifth centuries after Christ the Celts were displaced, first by Germans and finally by Slavs, who were moving westward from their original homeland in what is now southern Russia. The Slavs in turn had probably been given a strong push by tribes moving out of Central Asia, tribes with such exotic names as Tartars, Avars, Magyars and Khazars.

Bohemia was as far west as the Slavs were able to penetrate, and tradition says that the groups which arrived there took the name of the leader who had brought them—Czech. That is why if you look for Bohemia on a modern map, you won't find it. It's the *Czech* part of Czechoslovakia, the round, western end of the country just north of Austria, with Prague as its capital.

The fact that the Czechs are a Slavic people surrounded on most of three sides by Germans provides an explanation for much of their history. It is part of the larger story of an enduring antagonism between German and Slav which has lasted down to our own day. The assassination of an Austrian archduke by a Serbian (Slav) student to begin World War I, the Russian Revolution supported and encouraged by Prussia, Hitler's invasion of the Soviet Union and Stalin's consequent retaliation on Germany, may all be thought of as recent chapters in a long and bloody story.

Being the spearhead, in a sense, of the Slavic advance into the West, the Czechs have usually been the first to feel German pressure, and in fact have spent most of their history under some sort of German domination or influence. Except for a few scattered periods of independence, Bohemia was officially part of the Holy Roman (German) Empire from the late tenth century, though she did manage to preserve many of her native customs intact. From 1085 on, the dukes of Bohemia were permitted to use the title of King, but the concession was made by a German emperor, Frederick Barbarossa. A few, very few, Bohemians did manage through the years to be elected Holy Roman Emperor, thus strengthening the bond with the German Empire. One of these, Charles IV, decreed in 1356 that henceforth the King of Bohemia should be one of the seven Electors who would choose future emperors.

In 1438 a Habsburg became emperor, a situation which would be repeated for the next four hundred years. Although the empire was badly shaken during the Protestant Reformation, Bohemia remained in the Catholic camp, thanks in great measure to the labors of the Jesuits. These intrepid missionaries were especially successful in preserving the ancient Faith in the countries of Central Europe by emphasizing devotion to Our Lady and by forming sodalities and confraternities in her honor. This practice would also be one of John Neumann's favorite methods to inspire his people in their faith.

And so Bohemia remained in the Austrian, Habsburg, German empire until 1918, when it became part of the new, independent Slavic state of Czechoslovakia. Twenty years later Germans were back again, though they did not stay very long. Since 1948 no one needs to be told that Big Slavic Brother in Moscow has been the protector of the Czechs. While many of them chafed under Habsburg, German rule when they had it, most Czechs today would probably be glad to have it back again in place of the Slavic, but Communist regime now in power. Thus are the ironies of history.

So much for the political history of John Neumann's homeland. In the matter of its conversion and Catholic life, the situation is somewhat different but not without significant parallels. Almost from their first entrance into Central Europe, the Slavs were dominated, in fact were brutally enslaved, by an Asiatic tribe called the Avars. One of the favorite battle-tactics of the Avars was to herd great masses of Slavs on foot toward the enemy, while they themselves waited behind on their horses for the propitious moment to attack. By using strategies like this, the Avars managed to make themselves obnoxious for about two hundred years, but toward the end of the eighth century they came up against a more formidable adversary.

In 791 Charlemagne trounced the Avars, whose power was centered near the Danube in what is now Austria, but the Avars continued to cause trouble. In 796, therefore, Charlemagne returned to Avar country. There was no need for a third trip. The Avars were crushed so completely that they actually disappeared from the European scene, and have not been heard from since.

With the road to the Slavs now open, Charlemagne, ever mindful of spreading the Catholic Faith in the territories under his control, set up the archbishoprics of Salzburg in Austria and Regensburg in Bavaria as centers for the missionary activity to convert the Slavs. The first missionaries were in all probability Irish and Scottish monks who had been laboring in Bavaria. They were followed by German missionaries, whose success was steady, but not spectacular.

Now politics entered in and began to confuse the situation. About the year 855, a local leader named Rostislav, who controlled most of Bohemia and

St. Wenceslaus, Patron of Bohemia

Moravia, the next province to the east, managed to shake himself loose from the Germans for a time. He decided that if he was going to be free of German political rule, it would be nice to be free of German ecclesiastical rule also, so he asked the pope to send him some Slavic-speaking missionaries. The pope was St. Nicholas I, one of the great pontiffs of the early Middle Ages, but he did not comply with Rostislav's request. Either he did not have any Slavic-speaking, non-German priests in Rome at the time, or he was unwilling to repudiate an arrangement which had been going on for the past fifty years.

Rostislav was not one to be put off easily, even by the pope, and so he applied to the eastern emperor at Constantinople to send him some missionaries who could speak the Slavic language, but who were not Germans. The emperor discovered that he had some men who fulfilled the requirements: two brothers, Cyril and Methodius, from Thessalonica in northern Greece. They were probably of Greek origin, but were conversant with the Slavic tongue. Cyril was already a priest, but Methodius was not yet ordained. They accepted the assignment, and while preparing to depart, Cyril developed an alphabet, based in part on the Greek alphabet, to translate the Bible into Slavonic, the language of the Slavs. Cyril made another important decision, which would have far-reaching implications later. He followed the practice of the eastern Church, and translated the liturgy, as well as the Scriptures, into Slavonic.

The two brothers and their companions arrived at

Rostislav's court in 863. Their mission was beginning to be successful when Rostislav committed a rather foolish blunder. With new missionaries at work in his territory, he ordered the German priests to depart, thus taking a difficult situation and making it impossible.

Already annoyed that Cyril and Methodius had come at all, and even more distressed that they were using Slavonic instead of Latin in the liturgy, the German missionaries appealed to Rome. With the status of their mission in some doubt, Cyril and Methodius went themselves to Rome in 867. By the time they arrived, Pope St. Nicholas had died, and had been succeeded by Adrian ii.

The whole affair was further complicated by the fact that the eastern emperor, Michael iii, who had sent Cyril and Methodius to the Slavs, had become involved in a schism with Rome along with his patriarch, Photius. Photius had been the teacher and close friend of Cyril, and so naturally Rome was interested to know where the two missionary brothers stood. They in reply made it very clear to Pope Adrian that they stood on the side of the Holy See, and the pope not only approved their mission to the Slavs, but also ratified the use of Slavonic in the liturgy. So also did Adrian's successor, John viii, but in the meantime Rostislav had lost his independence to the German, Louis of Bavaria, and the German missionaries had returned to Bohemia and Moravia.

St. Cyril died in Rome without ever returning to his mission, but Methodius did return in 870, having

Prague: the stone bridge over the river Moldau
[Original sketch by Helmut Krommer]

been made both priest and bishop by Pope Adrian himself. Methodius presented his credentials to the German bishops, and was promptly imprisoned by them in a monastery for about two years. It required a special papal legate from Rome before Methodius was released and permitted to resume his missionary work. When St. Methodius died in 885, the German bishops expelled his followers and assumed control again. Ultimately, the Holy See changed its decision on the use of Slavonic in the liturgy and enforced the use of Latin everywhere in the West, probably as a reaction to the policy of the eastern empire, which was drifting farther and farther from its allegiance to Rome and would finally break away completely.

In spite of all the jealous, petty persecutions outlined above, the Catholic Faith survived and spread through Bohemia and Moravia. There are always men and women who realize that the Faith is more important than those who preach it, or fail to preach it, and that God's eternal Truths transcend national and racial boundaries. We should never underestimate or forget the great unifying force that the Catholic Faith has been throughout its history. It has brought men together when nothing else could, and given them a sense of oneness and true brotherhood in Christ where no political or cultural similarities previously existed. When we speak therefore of the continual tension between German and Slav in a region like Bohemia, we must realize that when both were living truly Catholic and Christian lives, they could and did get along together in harmony and mutual respect. As with the Irish and the English, there may not have been many happy German-Czech alliances, but there were plenty of happy German-Czech marriages. It was from such a marriage that John Neumann came, as we shall see.

Besides Sts. Cyril and Methodius, there were other saints who lived and worked in Bohemia. Several deserve a brief mention. The national patron is St. Wenceslaus, of Christmas-carol fame, who ruled the country in the early tenth century, and died in 928. St. Wenceslaus' grandmother, Ludmilla, is also a saint. It was she who was in great measure responsible for Wenceslaus' early education and training in the Faith. St. Wenceslaus allowed his Christian principles to prevail and pursued a policy of friendship toward his German neighbors, but in doing so he aroused the bitter hostility of the die-hard Slavic party and was finally murdered by his own brother, Boleslaus, perhaps even with the connivance of his mother.

In the fourteenth century there is another saint of importance to our main story: John of Nepomuk, Nepomuk being the small town in Bohemia where he was born. He was a canon of the Cathedral in Prague, and a strong supporter of the archbishop in a dispute with the king, another Wenceslaus. Popular legend also says that St. John was the queen's confessor, and that the king, who was given to violent, jealous rages, suspected his wife of evil and demanded to know what she had told John in Confession. When John refused to violate the Seal of Confession, the king had him thrown, bound and gagged, from Prague's famous bridge into the river Moldau or Vltava, depending on whether you prefer its German or Czech name. This happened in 1393. Some modern scholars doubt the reason, but no one doubts the fact that John of Nepomuk was thrown off the bridge at the king's command. He is traditionally pictured with his finger to his lips as a sign that he did not violate his priestly obligation. He is also one of the patrons of Bohemia, and many Bohemian boys bore his name, using either the Czech form: Nepomuk, or the Latinized version preferred by the Germans: Nepomucene. John Nepomucene Neumann was one of the latter.

A German and a Czech name for the saints, a German and a Czech name for the rivers, a German and a Czech name for practically all the towns and cities—the story of Bohemia reflected in its speech. It is perhaps fitting that John Neumann should also be a combination of the two nationalities.

3

Beginnings

IN THE YEAR 1802 a young man of twenty-eight left his native Bavaria and moved east to seek his fortune in the Austro-Hungarian province of Bohemia. Philip Neumann was determined to withdraw, if possible, from the problems of wars and rumors of wars caused mostly by the genius and ambition of another young man named Napoleon Bonaparte. Neumann was a knitter of stockings, and he hoped to establish his trade in a region a little more peaceful than the one he was leaving. He settled finally in a rather small village with a big name, Prachatitz, located in southwest Bohemia about fifteen miles from the nearest major town, Budweis. Budweis at that time was probably the third largest town in Bohemia, and had had its own bishop since 1786. Somewhat to the northwest of Budweis lies Bohemia's second largest city, Pilsen, and if the names of these two towns sound familiar,

Philip Neumann
John Neumann's father

Wenzel Neumann
his brother

they should, for one of the principal crops of the region is hops, and the Czechs and Germans of Bohemia have been brewing and drinking fine beer for centuries.

Prachatitz is an old town, with medieval walls and gabled buildings, dominated by the parish church of St. James. During the Middle Ages it flowered briefly as a trading center, but by the time Philip Neumann arrived to begin a new life, Prachatitz had accepted its status as a small, quiet village in a predominantly agricultural area.

Shortly after his arrival in Prachatitz, Philip Neumann married a local girl, but in 1804 his wife died in childbirth together with their first baby. The following year Neumann married again, another local girl of Czech ancestry by the name of Agnes Lebis. They were eventually to have six children, four girls and two boys. Their third child and first boy was born March 28, 1811, and baptized (the same day he was born) with the name of John Nepomucene.

Though not wealthy, Philip Neumann was successful in his knitting business, and came to have three or four men working for him. He also served at various times on the town council. He governed his business as he governed his life, with strong Catholic principles of honesty and morality, and brought up his children in the same manner. His wife was also a strong and faithful Catholic, attending Mass daily, and often giving alms of food and clothing to her less fortunate neighbors. Morning and evening prayers, grace before meals, and the rosary were an accepted and unquestioned routine in the Neumann household. Throughout his life the rosary would be one of John Neumann's favorite devotions, along with a consuming love of Our Blessed Lady. When he died, his flock could think of no greater tribute to pay him than to call him "Servant of Mary." Although his mother was Czech, Czech was not the language of John Neumann's home. His native tongue was German, and while he learned to speak Czech fluently, it was for him a second language.

Those who look for unusual or miraculous events, even in the childhood of the saints, will be disappointed in the life of John Neumann. His family was no different from hundreds of other pious, good Catholic families for whom the Faith was the most important thing in their lives. It is true that Philip and Agnes Neumann brought up their children strictly—the story is that often a look was enough to correct one of their offspring who might be getting out of hand—but a childhood governed by strictness does not necessarily mean an unhappy one. Where love and justice abound, no childhood can rightly be called unhappy.

So it was with John Neumann's family. He had the usual adventures and misadventures of small boys, like falling through an open cellar door when he was three years old, and landing unharmed fifteen feet below. The guardian angels of small boys often have a lot to do.

By all accounts John was a quiet, serious boy—not morose, but quiet. He was diligent in his studies, and

Prachatitz: the house where John Neumann was born

therefore usually gained high marks, but we would not, perhaps, call him brilliant. He followed after his father, however, in his love of books and desire for knowledge. He became a great friend of the village priest, Father Peter Schmidt, who besides instructing John in his catechism, also introduced him to the wonders of the natural sciences, especially astronomy and botany.

In the early years of the nineteenth century the reception of the sacraments sometimes took a different order from what it usually does in our day. John Neumann made his first confession at the age of six. He was confirmed at eight, but did not receive his first Communion until he was nine. While it is true that he had a toy altar at home, and enjoyed a true spirit of prayer from his early youth, his vocation to the priesthood was not immediately apparent. As he himself wrote later in life: "I cannot say I felt a decided inclination to the priesthood in my childhood. It is true that I had an altar made of lead and that I served Mass almost every day, but the idea of being a priest was so exalted that it did not seem within my reach."

One thing that John Neumann did yearn for at this age, however, was the chance to continue his education. Not many boys in Prachatitz went beyond grammar school—in fact there was no higher school to go to in the village. If John were to go further in his studies, it would mean going to Budweis. Since this involved a journey of about fifteen miles, it would also mean living in Budweis during the school term, which ran from November first to the end of September. To prepare for the entrance examination for high school, or *gymnasium*, as it is called in German, John took Latin lessons from his friend, Father Schmidt, and in the fall of 1823 passed his test and was admitted to the Budweis gymnasium. He was twelve years old.

The school years in Europe are arranged differently from the system we have in the United States. The first, or grammar school, lasts from about age six to twelve, and the high school course from age twelve to eighteen, but the last two years are often equivalent to the first two years of our colleges.

The courses at the gymnasium included Latin, mathematics, history, geography, and Christian doctrine, to which John applied himself with varying degrees of intensity and varying degrees of success. The last two years emphasized the reading of Latin and Greek authors.

The elder Neumann made arrangements for his son to stay in Budweis with a family which was also in the knitting trade, but the conditions for study were far from ideal, so much so that John's marks declined to the point where his father seriously considered removing him from school and putting him to work. Fortunately for John and ultimately for the Church in America, Philip Neumann was persuaded to change his mind, and a combination of new quarters, more inspiring teachers and a little more application gave John by his last term in the gymnasium the highest marks he had obtained in his studies up to that time.

Portrait of John Neumann at the age of 10
[Painting by an itinerant artist]

Following his graduation from the gymnasium in 1829, young Neumann entered the Budweis Institute of Philosophy for two more years. He had not yet decided definitely on a career, but the two-year course in philosophy was a prerequisite for whatever advanced studies he would take afterwards. Besides philosophy, the course included religion, higher mathematics, natural sciences and Latin philology. His teachers were Cistercian monks from the monastery of Hohenfurt, and John remembered them with pleasure and admiration throughout his life. His marks were uniformly good, even in mathematics, which had previously been his weakest subject. His real accomplishment, however, was in the natural sciences, especially botany, the study of which he had begun with Father Schmidt back in Prachatitz. Botany would remain a hobby of John Neumann's all his life.

If it seems strange that Cistercian monks should leave their monastery to teach in the city, the answer lies in the fact that the Church in the Austro-Hungarian Empire was still recovering from the heavy hand of the Emperor Joseph II, even though he had died in 1790. The son of Maria Theresa had become thoroughly infected in his youth with the anti-religious Rationalism of the eighteenth century, and when he became sole ruler on the death of his mother in 1780, he began a policy designed to bring the Church into complete subjection to the State. He confiscated Church property, closed Catholic schools and institutions, and seriously curtailed the work of both the religious orders and the secular clergy. In the case of the Cistercians of Hohenfurt, he threatened to close their monastery completely unless they supplied at least five professors for the Budweis Institute of Philosophy, and this is how John Neumann gained them as teachers. "God writes straight with crooked lines" turns out to be true again and again.

Joseph ii's Austrian subjects attached to him the epithet, "Joseph the Sacristan," because he meddled so much in Church affairs, an example of the dry, caustic wit for which the Austrians, and especially the Viennese, are famous. After World War II, when the Russians erected a statue in Vienna of a Red Army soldier, the Austrians quietly named it "The Unknown Plunderer."

John Neumann was twenty years old when he finished his course at the Budweis Institute of Philosophy in 1831, and it was time for him to choose his career. His piety had never been demonstrative or unusual, but it was very deep and important in his life. He toyed for a while, however, with the idea of becoming a doctor. Besides, the seminary at Budweis was full, and only a few new students were admitted each year. The Neumanns had no particularly important friends whose recommendations would carry weight, so why bother to apply? Nevertheless, John's mother urged him to apply anyway. She sensed that he really did want to become a priest, and mothers generally have a pretty good idea of what is going on inside their children's minds. John took her advice and sent in his application. To his surprise, he was accepted, and the future course of his life was set. To those who might wonder if his mother had the religious vocation instead of John Neumann, the rest of his life provides the answer. It can happen, of course, that strong-willed parents persuade a child to enter a career he or she does not want, but the children seldom if ever achieve real eminence in their calling, and as for sanctity—all the great spiritual writers agree that *that* must be singularly fought for and singularly won.

4

Budweis and Prague

WE DO NOT KNOW exactly what John Neumann looked like when he entered the diocesan seminary on November 1, 1831. Besides the portrait we have of him as a child, only two photographs are known to exist, both taken when he was older. John Neumann's features, however, are probably familiar to almost everyone by now, and I shall avoid trying to analyze or describe them. I must confess that I have never been able to make anything out of written descriptions of how people look. Such phrases as "broad brow," "noble nose" and "firm chin" always conjure up in my mind a picture totally unlike the real article. Certainly one of the marvels of creation is the amazing diversity that God is able to put into the human face, especially when you consider how few parts He has available to move around.

Would you say that John Neumann was

handsome? The old saw about beauty being in the eye of the beholder has some validity, but I for one would not call him especially handsome. There is strength in his face to be sure, and character, plenty of it, but good looks? I leave it to the reader to judge for himself. Mother Seton, our first native saint, was by unanimous consent a real beauty, but I doubt if John Neumann would have been invited to Hollywood for a screen test. This is perhaps as it should be, for if sanctity were inextricably bound up with facial beauty, most of us would have to give up the struggle!

About one of John Neumann's physical attributes, however, there is no argument. He was short, very short, at least for a man. Some of his biographers say that he was five feet, four inches tall, but others insist that he was only five feet, two and a half inches. Now everyone knows that we have all been getting taller, we Americans anyway. The experts in Washington recently decided that today's average American male stands over two inches taller than his average colonial ancestor, but even at the start of the Republic five feet, four inches was on the short side, and five feet, two and a half inches decidedly so. Some short men feel very much discriminated against—the bouncers in most clubs will tell you it's the short ones who give them the most trouble—but there is no indication that John Neumann's size gave him any problems. It was part of God's will for him, and as far as we know he accepted it without complaint.

Neumann's years at the seminary were years of

intellectual and spiritual growth. Once he had made
his decision to become a priest, he was happy and
confident that he was following God's plan.
Physically, however, the Budweis seminary left much
to be desired. The main building and the church
attached to it were in the middle of the town, with
hardly any grounds. At one time it had been a
Capuchin monastery, but in 1786 it had become a
casualty in Joseph ii's dispute with the Church. The
bishop of Budweis finally regained possession in
1804, and converted the building, together with the
church of St. Ann attached to it, into the diocesan
seminary. It had at the time far more students than it
could easily accommodate, and for a while the
younger seminarians, including John Neumann, had
to live outside in rented rooms.

Nevertheless, the two years he spent at the Budweis
seminary were happy ones for John, and his marks
were about the highest he had ever achieved in his
studies. At the end of the first year he was rewarded
by being one of the few permitted to receive the
tonsure and minor orders.

The courses taught were the usual seminary
courses, and only one professor was still tainted with
the pro-government, anti-papal ideas which had
come to be known collectively as "Josephism" after
their illustrious and royal promoter. It was during
this time that John Neumann acquired a great love for
Sacred Scripture and biblical studies, a love he carried
with him throughout his life. He also began to
cultivate a special talent he had, a great facility with

languages, and he started during these two years to
study Italian and French.

Another factor entered about this time into John
Neumann's life—one which would be supremely important to his future—his interest in and his desire to
work as a missionary in America. He was deeply
influenced by the stories and reports sent back from
the United States by another Austrian subject of
Slavic origin, Father, later Bishop, Frederic Baraga. A
native of Slovenia rather than Bohemia, Baraga was
born in 1797. He had gone to Vienna to study law,
but had met there St. Clement Hofbauer, the famous
Redemptorist (about whom more later), and was
drawn toward the priesthood. In 1830, the year
before John Neumann entered the seminary, Father
Baraga had gone to the United States and volunteered
for service among the Ottawa and Chippewa Indians
of Michigan and Wisconsin. His trip had been paid
for by the Leopoldine Foundation, a group organized
to provide spiritual and material aid to the missions,
and patterned after its French counterpart, the
Society for the Propagation of the Faith. (The
somewhat unusual name *Leopoldine* was chosen to
honor the emperor's daughter.) Having been
sponsored by the Foundation, Father Baraga sent
them frequent reports of his labors and adventures.
These were published, and became a strong
inspiration to young seminarians like John Neumann
to devote their own lives to the missions.

Frederic Baraga spent thirty-seven years working
among the Indians and trappers of Upper Michigan

Bishop Frederic Baraga

and Wisconsin, enduring extreme hardships and sufferings to carry out his mission. He was named first bishop of the area in 1853, and issued his pastoral letters in the Chippewa language. He had already written a grammar, dictionary, prayer books and a catechism in Chippewa. He died in 1868, and the cause for his eventual canonization is under consideration by the Church. One saint helping another—Frederic Baraga got his vocation through St. Clement Mary Hofbauer and in turn inspired St. John Neumann.

Caught up in the enthusiasm of Father Baraga's adventures and sacrifices, Neumann and two of his friends at the seminary determined to offer themselves for the missions in America. Adalbert Schmidt and John Savel would change their minds later, but John Neumann would not. In his youthful ardor he began preparing himself for the rigors of the North American wilderness by cutting down on his food and spending entire nights outside in the cool fall air.

He realized too that if his missionary work were to bear fruit, he should cultivate his talent for languages, and so, to the four he already knew or was studying—German, Czech, Italian and French—he determined to add English and Spanish. This of course was in addition to the Latin and Greek which his seminary studies required.

It was this desire to add to his linguistic store for work in the missions that persuaded John Neumann to take the next step in his career. Each year the bishop of Budweis chose two seminarians to complete their studies at the larger, more prestigious seminary in Prague. Hoping to perfect his French and begin English, which was not taught at all in Budweis, John applied for the appointment and was nominated. He would spend the final two years of his seminary training in the metropolis and capital of Bohemia.

In 1833 Prague was already an ancient and beautiful city, vying with Budapest to be the second city of the Austro-Hungarian Empire. It was built on both sides of the river Moldau, the halves connected by the famous stone bridge with its two distinctive towers from which the first John Nepomucene had been thrown to martyrdom. Prague's great university, dating from 1348, was the oldest institution of higher learning in Central Europe, the first university "east of the Rhine and north of the Alps." Its four principal schools of theology, philosophy, medicine and law had a total of about three thousand students.

In spite of the university's great reputation, it proved to be a disappointment for John Neumann. First, English was not taught at all, and new regulations for seminary students, promulgated shortly after he arrived, prevented him from taking any course in French. He studied both languages, however, as well as Spanish, on his own and was doing well in all three, especially French, by the time he graduated in 1835.

Secondly, and more importantly, the professors in Prague were much more infected with the rationalistic, anti-papal sentiments than had been the teachers in Budweis. It is not easy to attend college and to be constantly at odds with your professors over points in their teaching. An experienced teacher in any field has definitely the upper hand, and you will take issue with him at your peril. John Neumann was not one to give up easily, however, when he thought he was right, and he fortified himself with the pro-papal, pro-Roman works of the two great Jesuit Doctors of the Church, St. Peter Canisius and St. Robert Bellarmine. He was in fact so impressed by these two saints that for a time he seriously considered entering the Society of Jesus.

We can readily imagine how the professors must have reacted, to have objections tossed at them by a young upstart with Canisius' catechism in one hand and Bellarmine's in the other, so it is not surprising that John Neumann's marks in some of his classes were not as outstanding as they had been in Budweis. The professors did not quite flunk him, however, and John completed his seminary course in the prescribed two years.

It was during his last year in Prague, beginning in the fall of 1834, that John Neumann began writing a spiritual diary or journal, which he kept up until his work in America became too arduous. This journal was a personal account of his spiritual progress, and was never intended for publication, but its 468 pages give us a picture of John Neumann's soul which nothing else could. They show us that he was no plaster saint, but that his virtue and sanctity came after a real struggle against temptations of every sort. These temptations had the effect that God often intends them to have. They made John Neumann truly humble, conscious of his own weakness and aware of how helpless we all are without God's grace to strengthen us. The journal also reveals to us how delicate was Neumann's conscience—not scrupulous, but intensely sensitive to anything, however slight, which might offend God. Coupled with this was an ardent desire for perfection to which many of the prayers and ejaculations John wrote down bear witness: "Give me the graces which will aid me to obtain the perfection which You desire." "I will endeavor to perfect myself, for such is Your Holy Will!" "Give light to my eyes, O my Jesus, that I may more clearly see the way to perfection." And to Our Lady: "Mother, I am a sinner but wish to perfect myself."

Just before graduation a rather strange offer was made to John Neumann, strange because it seems so inconsistent with all that had gone before. He was asked if he would accept a position as secretary in some sort of Imperial embassy or commission. He was not asked to forego his ordination, but to accept the post as a priest. The reason given was that the government was looking for a young man in the ordination class who was knowledgeable in French, Italian, and Spanish. Even the rector of the seminary urged Neumann to accept the post, and when John refused on the plea that he intended to devote his life as a missionary in America, the rector and the government officials who had made the offer were all supposedly very disappointed and a little angry that

Prachatitz, John Neumann's native village

young Neumann should turn down such a golden opportunity. Most of John Neumann's biographers pass over the incident with a mere recitation of the fact that the offer was made and that he refused it, but at the risk of seeming to make a big thing out of nothing, the whole affair appears to me to be a bit peculiar.

Was John Neumann the only young priest-to-be in the Austro-Hungarian Empire who knew French, Italian, and Spanish? It seems hardly likely. Why should they settle on him anyway? He was not from a wealthy or noble family; he was really only a country boy from a small town in southern Bohemia. Now country boys from small towns in the South have made themselves famous, but it takes some doing, usually a combination of a lot of ambition, hard work and luck—especially ambition. John Neumann was not at all in the class of urbane, sophisticated extroverts, who do everything possible to let the right people know they are available for jobs like secretaries to Imperial embassies. His French at this time was probably good, but his knowledge of Italian, Spanish and also English had come mostly from books, and he can hardly have been really fluent in any of them. Besides, his regular seminary studies had made him practically a bookworm. His ardent piety and delicate conscience are not generally the qualities governments look for in budding ambassadors. Altogether I cannot avoid asking the obvious question, What in the world got into those Imperial officials to offer the post to John Neumann?

Now that I have raised the problem, I must confess I really have no conclusive solution to offer. It may be that some high government official recognized John Neumann's inner quality and felt it would do the Empire good to have someone like that in its diplomatic service, but I think you will agree this is not very plausible. The only answer I can give, and I admit it is only speculation, is that this offer of prestige and worldly honor was a final temptation to John Neumann's pride, a temptation brought by persons who were not always in the habit of taking their inspirations and ideas from on high. "All these will I give you," said the devil to Our Lord, referring to the kingdoms of this world, "if falling down you will adore me." Had John Neumann accepted the government position, America would have lost a missionary, Philadelphia a bishop, and the Church probably a saint.

The hurdles were not all over yet, however. Unbelievable as its seems to us today, the Diocese of Budweis had too many priests, and the bishop, being old and in poor health, was in no hurry to ordain any more! Even though he had completed his theological studies, John Neumann was informed that his ordination was to be postponed—indefinitely.

Through the offices of Father Hermann Dichtl, a canon of the cathedral in Budweis, John Neumann had applied to be accepted as a priest of the Diocese of Philadelphia. Even though Bishop Francis Kenrick, coadjutor to Bishop Conwell of Philadelphia, had written asking for German-speaking priests to come to his diocese, Father Dichtl had received no reply to his letters. Therefore John Neumann was truly in a state of limbo—not able to be ordained in his own diocese, and not accepted by the American bishop to whom he had applied. His diary records what a great spiritual trial this was for him. He had not yet told his parents of his plans to go to the United States, and his one consolation at the thought of probably never seeing his family again was that he might at least be able to say his first Mass and give them his priestly blessing before he left. He was not to have that consolation.

5

A Priest Forever

JOHN NEUMANN'S HOMECOMING in July 1835 was not exactly what he had thought it would be. He was not yet a priest, and could give his family no date when he would become one. He was also faced with the difficult assignment of telling them about his plans to go to America. His family reacted to the news much as any close family would react: his father was shocked and a little angry; his sisters cried; his mother wanted to cry but did not, at least in front of her son. Everyone knew, however, that if this was the will of God, they must not stand in the way of its fulfillment.

John's next duty, after telling his family of his plans, was to call on his own bishop in Budweis. The bishop received him cordially, but would not give him any definite promise about his ordination. Nor would he consent to grant John any letter officially releasing him from the diocese. Canon Law required that this be done before another bishop could receive a new priest or priest-to-be into his own diocese, but no word had come from the United States that Philadelphia or any other diocese would accept John, and so the bishop hesitated to act.

As the summer months dragged into autumn and the autumn into winter, John Neumann could do nothing but wait—and wait. His only consolation was in visiting local shrines in his district and offering himself again to do whatever it was God had in mind for him.

Finally, in February 1836, John could wait no longer. He decided he would start for America and rely on God's Providence to help him obtain whatever permissions he lacked. On February 8 he quietly left home early in the morning. He avoided the tearful farewells by not telling anyone but one sister that he was leaving. In a rather formal letter to his parents he explained that he thought this was the best way to lessen the mutual pain of departure, but it must have hurt his parents deeply not to be able to say goodbye. In leaving so abruptly, however, John was following his father's instructions. The elder Neumann had said. "If you believe yourself called by God, we shall put no obstacle in your way, but you must not take leave of us." When he discovered his son had obeyed him literally, Philip Neumann probably regretted his words, but it was too late to recall them. John would never see his mother again in this life, though he would see his father years later.

John Neumann's first stop was the home of his

New York Harbor, about 1836

bishop in Budweis. He received the bishop's blessing and presumably his permission to go to America, but still no official letter of release. John had about two hundred francs (about forty dollars) for his journey, part a donation from some of the priests of his district, and part what he had been able to put together himself.

Accustomed as we are today to rapid travel and tight schedules, it seems unbelievable that John Neumann took so long in getting from Bohemia to the coast of France. He did not actually sail for America until April 20, two and one half months from the day he had left home. He stopped first in Linz, Austria, where he received encouragement for his trip, then in Munich in Bavaria, where he received discouragement. He was told that Philadelphia had already found a pair of German-speaking priests, and therefore the call for his services had been withdrawn.

Philadelphia, however, was not the only American diocese in need of priests. Far from it. Priests John Neumann met along the way made various suggestions about where to apply, but since he did not have that all-important letter from his bishop, they were somewhat reluctant to go too far with him: after all, they could not be sure what kind of man they had on their hands. If they had only known!

Finally, in Strassburg, a priest agreed to write in John's behalf to Bishop Dubois of New York, but he could make no promises. John, however, was determined not to turn back. He had come this far in simple reliance on God's Providence, and he would continue his journey to the end. He moved on to Paris where he stayed a full month, hoping to get some definite commitment, but none came.

Paris is a city of great contrasts, religiously as well as in other ways. You will see libertines rubbing elbows with saints, and once in a while even becoming saints! John Neumann was amazed at the City of Light, but he was edified also to see people of all sorts and conditions crowding the churches during Lent and Holy Week.

Two days after Easter he decided he could wait no longer. He missed the Tuesday coach to Le Havre and ended up walking part of the way, but he arrived, nevertheless.

The ship which carried him across the Atlantic was the *Europa*, a large three-masted sailing vessel. Not until 1838, two years later, would steamships begin to make regular crossings of the Atlantic. The passengers included more than two hundred German and Swiss immigrants to America. Not all were Catholics, and some openly sneered at John's devotions, but he curbed his temper and continued his prayers. The voyage lasted forty days. At one point during a very strong wind John was standing alone on deck. He heard an interior voice telling him to move away, and as he did so, a part of the rigging came crashing down on the exact spot where he had been standing. He often told this story about himself, as proof that God's Providence is constantly watching over and protecting us.

The day John Neumann stepped ashore in New

New York, about 1836
[*View looking down Broadway toward the Battery*]

York was the feast of Corpus Christi, June 2, 1836. His clothes were in tatters and he had about one dollar left in his pocket, but he had finally arrived. He walked the streets of New York all day, eventually locating an inn where the proprietor spoke German, and where he could spend the night. The next day he sought out a German priest, Father John Raffeiner, and told him his story.

Now at last John's sorrow and frustration turned to joy. Father Raffeiner told him yes, they had heard about him from the priest in Strassburg; yes, he was welcome in New York; and yes, he was sure the bishop would ordain him. The next day John met Bishop John Dubois, who felt this young man was an answer to his prayers. He badly needed not one but several German-speaking priests to help care for the steady flow of immigrants pouring into New York, a city which had grown to 300,000 inhabitants and had out-distanced Philadelphia to become the largest city in the new Republic. When John explained that he lacked a letter from his own bishop, Bishop Dubois swept the objection aside, and said, "I can and must ordain you quickly, for I need you." The fact that he did not have his bishop's permission to be ordained and to serve in another diocese would be a source of concern to the delicate conscience of John Neumann in the future, but he had waited so long to hear the words Bishop Dubois spoke that now only joy filled his soul. So grateful was he to Our Lady that he promised to say a Rosary every day of his life in thanksgiving.

By accepting and ordaining John Neumann, Bishop John Dubois achieved a singular distinction. Years before he had been closely associated with our first native American saint, Mother Seton, helping her establish her community in Emmitsburg, Maryland; now he was to be instrumental in the life and work of our first male saint—a strange and wonderful coincidence indeed!

The ordination of her priests is one of the most impressive ceremonies the Church has in her magnificent liturgy. "You are a priest forever, according to the order of Melchisedech," she tells her sons, in commemoration of the mysterious figure in the Old Testament who offered bread and wine to God, and then is heard of no more. For John Neumann this supreme day of his life was June 25, 1836. The place was St. Patrick's Cathedral, not today's beautiful edifice on Fifth Avenue, but the old St. Patrick's, downtown on Mott Street, much less grand and impressive than its famous successor. Neumann was twenty-five years old. In gratitude for the wonderful gift God had given him, he wrote the following prayer in his diary the day after his ordination:

O Jesus, You poured out the fullness of your grace over me yesterday. You made me a priest and gave me the power to offer You up to God. Ah! God! This is too much for my soul! Angels of God, all you saints of heaven, come down and adore my Jesus, because what my heart says is only the imperfect echo of what Holy Church tells me to say.... I will pray to You (O Lord) that You may give to me holiness, and to all the living and the dead, pardon, that some day we may all be together with You, our dearest God!

There could be little time for rejoicing, however. The needs of the diocese were enormous, and three days after his ordination John Neumann was on his way to his first assignment—assistant to the old Father John Nicholas Mertz, and the younger but not-too-well Father Alexander Pax in the district around Buffalo.

Bishop John Dubois

6

Missionary Pastor

THE DIOCESE OF NEW YORK was one of the oldest in the country, established in 1808 along with Boston, Philadelphia and Bardstown, Kentucky, when Bishop John Carroll's original Diocese of Baltimore was first divided. In 1836 Bishop Dubois' territory included the entire state of New York and the northern one-third of New Jersey. It was the fastest-growing area in the country, and there were already 200,000 Catholics whose spiritual needs had to be cared for. To serve his people, Bishop Dubois had thirty-six priests, of whom thirty-one were Irish and three German. Almost daily, ships arrived in New York bringing more immigrants to swell the number of those already there, and so it is no wonder that the bishop was willing to dispense with some of the technicalities of Canon Law in order to gain a new priest for his diocese.

John Neumann's trip to Buffalo would be made almost entirely by water. He would sail up the Hudson River to Albany and then west by way of the Erie Canal.

The Erie Canal was the greatest engineering feat of the new United States. It was the longest man-made waterway in the world, and the pride and joy of DeWitt Clinton's term as governor of New York.

Before DeWitt Clinton became governor, back in 1808 when the Diocese of New York was first established, he had been mayor of New York City, and had been connected with a case which was to have very great implications for the progress of the Church in this country. The first bishop to be named for New York was an Irish Dominican then stationed in Rome, Father Luke Concanen. On his way to the United States to take possession of his diocese, Bishop Concanen died in Ireland, and so never actually ruled the Diocese of New York. In his absence, and before a new bishop could be appointed, the diocese was administered by Father Anthony Kohlmann, a learned and highly respected former Jesuit, who had been sent to New York by Bishop Carroll for the same reason John Neumann had come to America: to care for the German-speaking immigrants.

When we say that Father Kohlmann was a *former* Jesuit, it is not in any sense a reflection on his priestly character. The Society of Jesus had been suppressed by Pope Clement xiv in 1773 and was not restored until 1814. Many of the early missionaries in this country, including John Carroll himself, the first

Traveling on the Erie Canal, about 1836

bishop to be named for the United States, had been Jesuits in Europe who were forced to seek other fields for their priestly work.

During Father Kohlmann's term as administrator for the Diocese of New York, a man was suspected of having committed a serious theft. He was known to be a Catholic and was observed going to confession. Shortly afterwards he made restitution of the stolen property, but this was not definite proof that he had committed the crime, and so Father Kohlmann, his confessor, was summoned into court to give testimony. Father Kohlmann explained that one of the most serious obligations placed upon a Catholic priest is that of the Seal of Confession, and that under no circumstances may any priest reveal what he has been told by a penitent in the confessional. In the Middle Ages, of course, this fact was known and honored in all the courts in England as well as in other Christian countries, and no judge or lawyer would even think of asking a priest to reveal what he heard in confession. However, during Reformation times this privilege granted to priests was abolished in English law. The courts in the newly-formed United States naturally used the precedents of English law until the American legal system could develop its own precedents, and this was the first time such a case had come up since the new Republic was founded. Since the case had important political implications, it soon found its way to Mayor DeWitt Clinton. After listening to Father Kohlmann's explanation of a priest's obligation to keep the secret of confession, Clinton decided that Father Kohlmann could not be

compelled to testify. Such a decision was of course
crucial for the development of the Catholic Church in
America. For Mayor Clinton to rule as he did, and to
respect one of the most solemn obligations placed on
a Catholic priest, is eternally to his credit.

The Erie Canal was completed in 1825, eleven years
before John Neumann's arrival in America. Called
half in jest and half in admiration, "Clinton's long
ditch," it ran for 363 miles, and its eighty-three stone
locks raised a boat over five hundred feet, from the
level of the Hudson River at the eastern end to that of
Lake Erie and Buffalo in the west. The canal boats
were pulled by horses walking along the banks, and
the average speed was between three and four miles
per hour. The Erie Canal was more than just an
interesting statistic, however. It quickly became the
main route west for thousands of people, and opened
up the entire Great Lakes region to settlement and
development. Within a few years after it was opened,
more than twenty thousand boats a year plied its
waters.

The canal boat on which John Neumann traveled to
Buffalo was typical of its class. It had three-decker
bunks for forty-eight passangers and five crewmen,
but the number actually traveling on the boat was
closer to ninety. In the morning the bunks were
folded away and the large cabin transformed into a
combination dining- and sitting-area for the remain-
der of the day.

Father Neumann had been instructed by Bishop
Dubois to interrupt his journey at Rochester for a

The Erie Canal: locks at Lockport, New York

short period of time in order to aid the German
Catholics who were living there. He arrived on the
Fourth of July to the accompaniment of bonfires and
cannons celebrating the nation's sixtieth birthday.
Most of the Catholics in Rochester at this time were
Irish, as was the pastor, Father Bernard O'Reilly, but
there was already a substantial number of German
Catholics as well.

The early bishops in the United States had a very
real problem when great numbers of immigrants
began arriving who did not speak English. The
newcomers could not communicate with their priest
nor the priest with them, and there was a serious
danger that they and their children would be lost to
the Church. In John Neumann's day the most pressing
need was for priests who spoke German, and he and
others like him filled a vital need. Later in the century
other nationalities began arriving, and missionaries
like St. Frances Xavier Cabrini were urged by Pope
Leo xiii to go, not to the Far East, but to America in
order to work with Italian immigrants, but in the
early years it was the Germans who were coming in
the greatest numbers.

Father O'Reilly was delighted to have the assistance
of a German-speaking priest, even if it was to be for
only a short time, and he and Father Neumann began
a life-long friendship. Fourteen years later, in 1850,
Father O'Reilly was made Coadjutor Bishop of Hart-
ford, and in 1852 succeeded to the See. That same
year he assisted at the consecration of John Neumann
as Bishop of Philadelphia, and so the careers of the
two men bear a certain similarity. Their deaths,

however, were not similar. Bishop O'Reilly was lost at sea when the ship on which he was returning from Europe sank in 1856, leaving no survivors.

Along with their pastor, the Germans in Rochester received Father Neumann with enthusiam, and he set about at once administering the sacraments and instructing both adults and children in their Faith. As he began his priestly work, a work to which he dedicated his life, he wrote this prayer to Our Lord in his diary:

My Lord and my God! Have mercy on me and those sheep who, for the time being, have been entrusted to me. Give to my tongue words of life. Purify their hearts and make them heed all sound advice and every admonition. Your grace must do everything because I can do nothing but sin—O Jesus, my Redeemer, I am taking Your place. Let me be a redeemer for this parish!

The first time he baptized a child was an occasion of immense joy for him, and he wrote: "If the child baptized today dies in the grace of this sacrament, then my journey to America has been repaid a million times, even though I do nothing for the rest of my life."

Father Neumann was able to stay in Rochester only a few days, but before he left for Buffalo he met a priest who was to have great influence on his life. Father Joseph Prost was one of a small band of Redemptorist priests who had begun laboring in America with the German-speaking immigrants. He returned to Rochester just as John Neumann was about to leave. Neumann was very much impressed

by the older man, and the seed was sown which four
years later would inspire him to apply for admission
into the Redemptorists. For the present, however, his
assignment was Buffalo and he arrived there on July
12.

The Erie Canal had turned Buffalo into a true boom
town. It boasted a population of 16,000 people, the
latest New York fashions, a new theatre and kerosene
lamps to light the streets at night. Only one of those
streets was paved, however, for one-fifth of a mile.
From the photographs made later of the boom towns
of our last frontier, Alaska, we get some idea of what
life in Buffalo must have been like in 1836. The one
outstanding feature of these towns, at least during
certain periods of the year, was mud—oceans of
it—constantly churned up by the traffic of horses and
wagons. When we read that our ancestors went
around all day in high boots, we know the reason
why.

As John Neumann arrived to take up his duties in
Buffalo, the elderly pastor, Father John Mertz, was
away in Europe on a much-needed vacation, if you
consider raising funds for his people to be a vacation.
The parish was in the care of Father Mertz's assistant,
Father Alexander Pax, who had been in Buffalo
himself only one year. So delighted was he to see
Father Neumann that he offered him his choice of
assignment, either caring for the Catholics in the city
itself or in the four unfinished parishes in the area
around Buffalo. Father Neumann chose the latter.
The area which he had under his charge amounted to

Buffalo: North West view, about 1836

no less than nine hundred square miles. There was a small church to the north of Buffalo in the village of North Bush near the present city of Kenmore. Another was in Williamsville to the northeast. A third was in Cayuga Creek, and the fourth was thirty miles south at Eden.

Since Williamsville seemed to be the most central, Father Neumann chose that as his residence. Besides, while the other three churches were of wood, Williamsville had a stone church, or at least the beginnings of one. The story goes that the land had been donated by a Protestant some years before who had come to dislike his Protestant pastor. He had offered land for a church to the Catholics on condition that they would build a stone church larger and more beautiful than the local Protestant meetinghouse. Father Mertz had accepted the gift and the conditions attached to it, but the church was a long way from completion. There was of course no such thing as a rectory, and so Father Neumann lived for a while in the local inn, owned by a Catholic German named Jacob Wirtz.

The total number of Catholic families in the area under John Neumann's care amounted to about four hundred, of whom three hundred were German, and the rest Irish, French and Scotch. There were hardly any roads worthy of the name in the district, and so Father Neumann's trips to his various missions took anywhere from two to twelve hours. When he arrived in Williamsville, the stone church had its walls erected but as yet had no roof. On the day of his first

Mass in the church, the local bigots gathered outside and threw stones over the walls, one of them landing on the altar. This was John Neumann's first reception to his new parish, but in general he was not molested in his work by the Protestants of the area. More trouble came from his own parishoners. The German immigrants were frugal and hard-working, but they were also strong-willed and independent. A recent writer has remarked that it was only the strong-willed and independent ones who had the courage to pull up stakes and leave their native land to start life again in a new and undeveloped country, but they carried this independence over into their religious life as well.

The legal status even of the Catholic churches during the early years of this country was in accordance with the practice common to most of the Protestant churches. Title to the church property and building was vested in a board of lay trustees, not in the pastor or the bishop. In the Protestant congregations the trustees could dismiss the minister almost at will, and while this was not the case among the Catholics, some of the more strong-willed trustees acted sometimes as though it were. Clashes between the pastor and the trustees were frequent and often bitter, and the problem of trusteeism plagued the Church in America for many years. Father Neumann's problems with his own trustees were not so serious, but their high-handed attitude did at times cause him trouble.

Besides saying Mass and administering the sacraments, one of Neumann's chief concerns was instructing the young children in the Faith. All his life this was one of his favorite priestly duties, and he had a special gift for teaching children. He was not above giving small rewards for lessons faithfully learned, and many small holy pictures and pieces of candy found their way from the pastor's pocket into the pockets of his charges.

Though Father Neumann preferred to make his rounds on foot, he was eventually persuaded by his parishioners to accept the gift of a horse. He was thrown more than once, but he finally succeeded in learning to ride, though never really well. He and the horse ultimately became quite attached to one another, although on one occasion the latter succeeded in gobbling down a whole collection of botanical specimens Father Neumann was preparing to send to Bohemia.

Being, as we have said, strong-willed and independent people, the parishioners often managed to get into arguments with one another, and they took their grievances to the pastor, expecting him to take sides. Father Neumann devised an effective way to reduce the number of complaints. "Let us first say the stations of the cross or the rosary," he would say, "and then we shall talk over the matter." Not all were willing to put in the preliminary fifteen or twenty minutes of prayer the pastor suggested, and those who did usually found that their anger had subsided by the time the prayers were over.

In 1837 Father Neumann decided to change his residence from Williamsville to North Bush. New arrivals had moved the center of population somewhat, but more important was the fact that Jacob Wirtz was a little difficult to live with. Being the pastor's host had given Mr. Wirtz a feeling of some importance, and it was not a situation Father Neumann wished to encourage. Besides, in moving to a new location, it would give him an opportunity to begin what he really wanted and needed—a rectory of his own.

Shortly after settling in North Bush, Father Neumann was honored by a visit from Bishop Dubois. Although eighty years old at the time, the bishop was determined to visit his diocese. Father Neumann's parishioners gave him a royal welcome, and the aged bishop was not only delighted at the reception he received, but also impressed by how much the young priest had been able to accomplish in just one year. The dinner given for the bishop was a great success, even though the ladies of the parish had to gather up the dishes at the end of each course and hustle them off to be washed so that they could be used again for the next one.

It was a happy day for John Neumann when he was able to move into his own two-room, log-cabin rectory. It was hardly palatial. The furniture consisted of four chairs and two old battered trunks, but it gave him privacy for his work and personal devotions which he could never have at Jacob Wirtz's inn. He began cooking his own meals, but often did not bother, and once went for four weeks living on bread alone. Throughout his term as pastor, Father

Log chapel of the type built by St. John Neumann

Neumann tried never to be a burden on his people. He knew that most of them were desperately poor, and though on his parish rounds he would never refuse a meal if it were offered to him, he was never known to ask for one.

He was always on the move. He traveled northwest as far as Niagara Falls and east as far as Batavia, anywhere, in fact, where he could visit a group of Catholics and bring them the sacraments and the consolations of their Faith. On one of his trips he was given a ride by a Protestant preacher, and when the man discovered he was talking to the priest of the district, he asked Father Neumann if he would participate in a public debate. Neumann finally consented, but the preacher had taken on more than he had bargained for. Despite his worn clothes and humble appearance, John Neumann was thoroughly versed in Holy Scripture, philosophy, theology and Church history, and he was more than a match for the preacher's home-grown approach to religion. He was not invited again to debate the merits of his Church in public.

As the number of German immigrants to the United States continued to increase without any sign of abatement, Father Neumann began writing letters to priests he had known in Europe, asking them to do whatever they could to inspire more German-speaking missionaries to come to America. No priests came to assist him, but in September 1839 his own brother, Wenceslaus, or Wenzel, arrived to be his helper. Wenzel was not a priest and would never become

one, but he was a good teacher, and he assumed
many of his brother's teaching and catechetical
duties. Wenzel also did the cooking, and the quality
of Father Neumann's meals improved considerably.

Eventually a new German-speaking priest did
arrive, sent by Bishop Dubois to help Father
Neumann in his work, but unfortunately, things did
not work out as planned. By far the great, great
majority of priests who came to the United States
were zealous, hardworking missionaries willing to
sacrifice themselves for the salvation of souls and the
glory of God, much as John Neumann had done, but
occasionally there would come one who was not. It
was only natural that once in a while a bishop in
Europe would send off to America a priest with
whom he was having trouble. Some of these men
turned out well, but some turned out to be as much of
a problem to their new bishop as they had been to the
old one. Such, unfortunately, was the case with the
new priest who arrived to help Father Neumann. He
was stationed at Williamsville, but his activities there
aroused the displeasure of the bishop, and he was
ordered to leave. He refused and appealed to the
trustees. It was in cases like this that the evils of
trusteeism were most apparent. If the trustees sided
with the recalcitrant priest against the bishop, a
whole parish might be split off from the Church. In
this particular instance there was no schism, but it
took the combined efforts of Fathers Neumann, Mertz
and Pax to persuade the parishioners in Williamsville
to obey the proper ecclesiastical authorities and reject

the dissident priest.

Despite Father Neumann's seemingly endless labors during these years, he was careful always to take care of his own spiritual life. He proposed the following schedule for himself and followed it as closely as he could. The time before Mass was devoted to meditation and private prayer. The hours from nine to eleven he spent teaching catechism to the children, and then allowed one more hour for recreation with them. After lunch he would prepare his sermons and then teach again from two to four o'clock. In reciting his breviary, he said Matins before he retired in the evening, Lauds in the morning when he got up, Prime before Mass and Terce afterwards. Sext and None he recited in the church at noon, and Vespers and Compline in the same place at six in the evening. He resolved to cultivate holy silence and to deny himself as many earthly pleasures as he could, so that his preaching might be more acceptable to his parishioners and more profitable to their salvation.

Despite these resolutions, however, and despite the fact that he labored tirelessly for his flock, Father Neumann felt that he was becoming less and less fervent in the service of God. He experienced long periods of dryness in his prayers, and his delicate conscience made him accuse himself of pride and sloth where most observers would have agreed that just the opposite was true. Like all the saints, he considered himself a useless and unprofitable servant, and unworthy of God's grace.

In 1838 Father Neumann visited Rochester for a few days, and had an opportunity to talk again with Father Joseph Prost, the Redemptorist. Neumann was still impressed by the zeal of this holy priest, and by the religious life he was leading.

In the summer of 1840, in spite of the fact that his brother Wenzel was on hand to assist him, Father Neumann had a complete breakdown in health as a result of his labors, and during the three months that it took him to recover, he thought and prayed seriously about his vocation. He discussed it with Father Pax, who was then his confessor, and after a period of many months, Father Pax advised him that it was his opinion that John Neumann should become a religious.

On September 4, 1840, therefore, Father Neumann wrote to Father Prost, who had in the meantime become Redemptorist superior in America, and was then living in Baltimore, and applied for admission into the Congregation of the Most Holy Redeemer. He explained his action in a letter which he wrote later to his parents: "I think that this is the best thing I can do for the security of my salvation. The constant supervision of religious superiors and the good example of fellow religious spur one to lead a life more pleasing to God than one can lead in the world."

Father Prost had recognized John Neumann's quality for a long time and wrote an immediate and favorable reply. On September 16, Neumann applied to Bishop John Hughes, the administrator of the Diocese of New York following the death of Bishop

Dubois, and asked for permission to leave the secular priesthood for the Redemptorists. Bishop Hughes was well aware of Father Neumann's work and was naturally reluctant to release him, but Father Prost interceded, and the bishop finally agreed.

Early in October, John Neumann bade goodbye to his friends and parishoners in North Bush and started for Pittsburgh to enter the Redemptorist novitiate. A short time later his brother Wenzel followed, having put Father Neumann's affairs in order, and applied for admission into the same Congregation.

7

Son of St. Alphonsus

THE CONGREGATION OF THE MOST HOLY REDEEMER had been founded in the Kingdom of Naples in 1732 by St. Alphonsus Maria de Liguori. Alphonsus was born of a noble family and was beginning his career as a lawyer, when he lost an important case to a clever opponent and decided to devote his life to God instead of to the law. Becoming a priest, he realized that many people living in isolated country districts were not being adequately cared for by the Church, and he founded a congregation of priests dedicated to this purpose. St. Alphonsus was a brilliant theologian and spiritual writer. His treatise on moral theology became a standard authority throughout the world, and his devotional writings, particularly *The Glories of Mary* and *The Way of Salvation*, have been an inspiration to thousands of souls. Though his health was not at all good during much of his life, he lived to

St. Alphonsus Maria de Liguori

the age of ninety and did not die until 1787. St. Alphonsus was canonized in 1839 and proclaimed a Doctor of the Universal Church in 1871.

Despite the fact that he lived fifty-five years after founding it, the Congregation of the Most Holy Redeemer did not seem to prosper during St. Alphonsus' lifetime. In fact, his last years were saddened by a serious dissension within his Order. As an old man in failing health, he was persuaded, really tricked, into accepting a new set of Constitutions demanded by the king of Naples. When the revised Rule was condemned by the pope, St. Alphonsus was technically outside the Order he had founded, and died before the matter was settled.

God did not permit the Redemptorists to wither away, however. A young man, a Bohemian like John Neumann, joined the Order in 1784, and carried its mission and spirit with him back across the Alps. St. Clement Mary Hofbauer's zeal and energy made him almost the second founder of the Redemptorists, and his labors for the Faith in the Imperial capital earned for him the title: *Apostle of Vienna.* When he died in 1820, he had laid the foundations for a strong and vigorous Order, and under his able successor, the Venerable Father Joseph Passerat, the German and Austrian branches of the Redemptorists expanded throughout Europe and finally to America. In 1832 three priests and three brothers arrived to begin the work of the Order in the United States, invited by Bishop Fenwick of Cincinnati. So successful were they to become in dealing with the German-speaking

Catholics, even in parishes seething with discontent, that Archbishop Samuel Eccleston of Baltimore suggested at one point that all the German parishes in the United States be given into the charge of the Redemptorists. It was neither possible nor practicable to adopt this suggestion, but the idea indicated the esteem in which the fathers of the Congregation were held by the American bishops.

The German Catholics were not really disloyal to the Church, but they needed priests who understood their problems and who could preach to them in their own language. This need the Redemptorist Fathers ably fulfilled. In 1840, when John Neumann applied for admission into the Redemptorists, they had in the United States four permanent foundations: St. Philomena's Church in Pittsburgh, St. John's in Baltimore, St. Joseph's in Rochester and St. Alphonsus' in Norwalk, Ohio. It was to St. Philomena's that John Neumann was ordered to report to begin his novitiate. Except for one man who had asked to join as a lay brother, Neumann was the first novice to enter the Redemptorist Order in the United States.

He had applied for admission into the Redemptorists in the hope that he would be able to give himself to prayer and meditation, at least for a time, but this was not to be. He arrived in Pittsburgh early on a Sunday morning, and his first assignment was to sing the High Mass and to preach the sermon! Throughout his life Father Neumann never possessed a good singing voice, and it is not recorded what the parish thought of his first High Mass as a Redemp-

Pittsburgh and its "Golden Triangle" in the mid-19th century

torist, but nevertheless he did as he was instructed. The demands on the Fathers' services were unending, and the fact that John Neumann was already a priest made it almost impossible for him to have the quiet, peaceful novitiate he so much desired. He was to say later in life that he really had had no novitiate, and in fact during his first year as a Redemptorist he moved his residence no less than eight times. The ceaseless activity could not fail to take its toll on Father Neumann's spirit, and there were many times during his first year as a Redemptorist when he seriously questioned his decision to enter the Order. Years later he listed for his nephew, John Berger, who was then himself a Redemptorist novice, the kinds of temptations he had experienced in this first year:

One novice imagines himself deficient in physical strength; another deludes himself with the notion that things would go more smoothly in another Order, or that he could possibly do more good for the honor of God while living in the world. Sadness and melancholy seize upon some while others are beset by a love of their own ease. Some are attacked by homesickness, or other temptations born of self-will, disgust for prayer, want of confidence in their superiors, and so forth. The temptations of the soul are doubtless as numerous as the disorders of the body, but to remain steadfast and to persevere in all this turmoil of spirit, there is no better remedy than prayer to the Blessed Virgin for the grace of perseverance. At the same time, immediate disclosure of the temptation to one's director is absolutely necessary.

It is easy for us to assume, when we first encounter the saints, that they were men and women of unwavering virtue and steadfast purpose who never stumbled in their drive toward sanctity. In the life of St. John Neumann, however, we see that such was not the case. The fact that he endured and conquered temptations, doubts about his vocation, sadness and darkness of mind and spirit should be a consolation and inspiration to all who strive to walk in the way of God's grace.

Toward the end of 1841, however, it became clear to the Redemptorist superiors that if Father Neumann were not given some respite from his labors, he might very well be lost to the Congregation, and so he was ordered to report to the Provincial House in Baltimore. Here, for five weeks at least, he had rest from his work and a chance to make a long retreat. His doubts were laid to rest and his temptations conquered, and on January 16, 1842, at the age of thirty-one, he made his profession as a member of the Congregation of the Most Holy Redeemer.

Since he was the first Redemptorist novice in America, he was also the first Redemptorist to be professed. Now he could write to his parents:

I now belong to it (the Redemptorist Order) body and soul. The mutual bodily and spiritual help, edification and good example, which one has around him till his death in such a spiritual society, make my life and my office a great deal easier for me. I also confidently hope that death in this society will not be unwelcome to me, as is generally the case with people of the world.

As soon as he was professed, his work began again in earnest. Besides tending to the needs of the German Catholics in the city, the Redemptorist Fathers radiated out through the countryside locating scattered German families and organizing them, whenever possible, into parishes. They were the Catholic circuit riders of their day. Father Neumann's exact itinerary during this time has not been preserved, but more than one country parish had on its register the name of John Neumann, C.SS.R., as the minister presiding at a marriage or a baptism.

About the time Neumann entered the Redemptorists, the Church of St. John had grown too small to take care of the needs of the German Catholics of Baltimore, so about seven months after his profession the cornerstone was laid for the new church of St. Alphonsus, still standing today. So impressive was it that for many years it was known as the German Cathedral of Baltimore. The parish became the center for a great spiritual renewal of the German Catholics. Many who had given up the practice of their Faith returned to it, and hardly a Sunday passed without one or two converts being received into the Church. At times there were as many as twenty or thirty under instruction.

John Neumann remained in Baltimore about two years, working in the main parish or taking his turn in visiting the outlying missions, but in March 1844 he was given a new assignment—pastor of the church where he had first entered the Redemptorist Order, St. Philomena's in Pittsburgh.

The Diocese of Pittsburgh had been erected just eight months previously, with Bishop Michael O'Connor as its first Ordinary. It embraced the western half of Pennsylvania, and included only about forty-five thousand Catholics, of whom twelve thousand were Germans, in a total population of 800,000. A new St. Philomena's Church had been begun but was not nearly completed, and Father Neumann as the new pastor was faced with the job of finishing the church and paying off the substantial debt already incurred. His people were poor, but he asked each parishioner to contribute five cents a week toward the building fund, and construction moved ahead. Father Neumann never knew from week to week whether he would have the money to pay the workmen on Saturday, but somehow God always seemed to provide. In later years Bishop O'Connor would say that Father Neumann had built a church without any money.

An amusing incident is told which illustrates the pastor's shrewdness in administering his building fund. A wealthy parishioner of St. Philomena's had made a loan to Father Neumann for the fund. Hearing a rumor that his investment was not safe, he appeared at the church one day and demanded his money. The money had long ago been used for building materials, and Father Neumann had nothing on hand to repay the loan on such short notice, but he faced his visitor with a smile. "Would you like your money in gold or silver?" The man was completely disarmed. "Oh, if that's the case," he said, "keep it, for it is safe with

Pittsburgh: St. Philomena's Church
[Built by St. John Neumann]

you." The church was finally dedicated in November 1846, and the debts paid to the last penny.

As always in John Neumann's career, the spiritual progress of his flock was his most important concern. There is something in the German temperament (Neumann said that it was in the American temperament!) which likes to join clubs and societies, and many of the irreligious and anti-Catholic organizations of the day made a strong appeal to the German immigrants. Father Neumann countered by establishing religious societies in the parish for his people to join. The Confraternity of the Sacred Hearts of Jesus and Mary, the Confraternity for a Happy Death, and the Confraternity of the Rosary were among those he organized and encouraged.

Throughout his life John Neumann's love of teaching the Faith to children never wavered, and it was during his years in Pittsburgh that he published in German his *Smaller Catechism*, his *Larger Catechism*, and his *Bible History*. All three went through several editions and were used for many years in German Catholic schools throughout the United States, but only the *Smaller Catechism* was ever translated into English.

As pastor, Father Neumann spent many hours in the confessional and insisted on taking all of the middle-of-the-night sick calls himself. His sermons were always directed to the needs of his parishioners—simple in language, but clear, ordered and filled with solid doctrine and devotion. As in Baltimore, there was a whole string of outlying missions and parishes to care for, and Father Neumann was fortunate in having two zealous and holy priests as his assistants: Father Francis Seelos and Father Joseph Mueller, ("the three saints at St. Philomena's," as they were called). The pastor, however, insisted on taking the most burdensome duties on his own shoulders.

As his three-year term drew to a close in 1847, his assistants were worried that Father Neumann's health was heading for a complete breakdown again. They confided their concern to the American Superior, and instead of being given a new assignment, Neumann was ordered to return to Baltimore.

In submission to the will of God, he returned prepared for any humble assignment which might be given him, but he was in for a surprise. Word had just come from the Provincial in Europe that Father John Neumann, C.SS.R., only five years a Redemptorist, had been named Superior of the Congregation in the United States.

8

Vice-Provincial

THE FIRST REDEMPTORIST FOUNDATIONS in the United States were under the direct supervision of the Order's Vicar-General and his consultors in Vienna. In 1844, however, during one of the Austrian government's periodic interferences in Church affairs, jurisdiction of the American houses was taken from Vienna and placed under the Provincial in Belgium. The Belgian Provincial, Father Frederick DeHeld, made a visit to his new subjects in 1845. He was much impressed by the progress that had been made, as anyone would be, but he was also concerned that the Order was expanding too rapidly in the United States. The 1840s saw a great rush of immigrants into this country, and the American bishops, desperate for priests and moved by the success the Redemptorists were having with German Catholics, were pressing them to establish more and more new parishes and to take over others which had a large German population. Some of the Fathers were eager to comply, but others were afraid that too rapid an expansion would divide the Congregation and dissipate its spirit. It was the same problem the Church has had since her foundation. "The harvest is great," Our Lord said, "but the laborers are few. Pray therefore the Lord of the harvest, that he send laborers into his harvest."

Workers are needed, but they must not allow their own spiritual life to suffer from too much activity. Father Joseph Passerat, the Redemptorist Vicar-General, was concerned that this might happen to some of his sons. In a circular letter written about this time he gave them sound advice:

> I say to you, beloved confreres, may you work with zeal for the salvation of souls. It is your vocation to serve abandoned souls. Great will be the merit and reward of this work if your own salvation is not thereby neglected. . . Work in itself, even the holiest work, can neither sanctify nor save us if one does not preserve the fervor of charity by the exercises of the spiritual life, and, indeed, through the exact observances of the prescriptions about such matters given in the holy rule. A St. Francis Xavier, a St. Francis de Sales, and a St. Vincent de Paul certainly worked much for the salvation of souls. But did these men while doing so much work feel themselves free from the exercises of the spiritual life?

Father DeHeld, the new Provincial, was firmly

committed to making haste slowly. He was perhaps
overly cautious and has been somewhat criticized for
not understanding fully the condition of the Church
or of the Redemptorist Order in the United States, but
until more priests could be sent to America, he absolutely forbade his subjects to incur any new debts or
to open any new houses, no matter what appeals were
made to them by the American bishops. In fact, two
new houses, one in Detroit and the other in Washington, D.C., which had been opened without his full
permission, he ordered closed.

John Neumann had experienced for himself the
spiritual dangers attendant upon too much activity,
and he was basically in agreement with the Provincial's views. He realized, however, that the assignment being given him, Superior of the American
houses, was an extremely difficult one. He was only
thirty-five years old, younger than many of the forty
priests now under him, some of whom had held
distinguished posts in the Order before coming to
America. His appointment was provisional, and his
authority severely limited. In such a situation it was
impossible to please everyone concerned. That John
Neumann accomplished his mission as well as he did
was a tribute to his zeal, his holiness, and his genuine
love for the Redemptorist Order, but his appointment
provided a severe test for his humility. He was given
explicit instructions as to what he could and could not
do, but he was not given the power to enforce his
decisions. Those who opposed the policy of
retrenchment either neglected to obey his instructions
or openly refused to do so, and insisted on their right

Baltimore: St. James' Redemptorist Church
[where St. John Neumann made his profession as a Redemptorist]

of appeal to Europe. During this period several priests left the Congregation, although they either joined other religious orders or remained as secular priests. None actually left the Church.

Several months after Father Neumann assumed the direction of the American Redemptorists, a new Visitor arrived from Europe, Father Martin Starck, sent by the Vicar-General in Vienna. The Austrians in general tended to take a more lenient view toward expansion than the Belgian Provincial, and Father Starck permitted new foundations to be made in Detroit and New Orleans.

When he left to return to Europe, the Visitor appointed two consultors to assist Father Neumann, one of whom seriously questioned Neumann's qualities as Superior and did not hesitate to say so. In the meantime Father DeHeld had decided that it would be a good idea for the American houses of the Redemptorist Order to be organized into a separate province of their own, and had suggested this to the officials in Vienna and Rome. Pending a decision, the American houses were to be taken away from the Belgian province and given back to the Austrian.

Early in 1848, Rome decided that the American houses would be erected not into a full province but into a vice-province, and so informed Father Passerat in Vienna. In March 1848, however, revolutions broke out all over Europe, and Father Passerat found himself in exile in Belgium without his consultors. Acting on his own authority, he wrote to John Neumann appointing him the new Vice-Provincial, but the rules of the Order demanded that such an appointment have the approval of the consultors. Since the consultors were now scattered all over Europe, the validity of Father Passerat's appointment was at best questionable, a fact that the new Belgian Provincial, Father DeHeld's successor, was quick to note. Inasmuch as final ratification of the transfer of the American houses from the Belgian province back to the Austrian had not come before Father Passerat left Vienna, the new Belgian Provincial, Father Michael Heilig, assumed he was still the Superior of the Redemptorists in the United States.

Imagine trying to be the local Superior in such a situation! Another man would have thrown up his hands in disgust, but John Neumann quietly accepted everything as another cross coming from the hands of a loving God. To those who urged that he defend himself against the unfounded complaints of a few dissidents, he replied: "Let it go. Do not be sorry for me. I have never done anything to become a superior and I will not do anything to remain one. On the contrary, I will thank God if I am relieved of this responsibility."

Accepting Father Heilig's claim to be the lawful Superior of the American houses, John Neumann wrote him in August 1848 asking humbly to be permitted to step down as Superior in America. Influenced in part by the complaints made against Father Neumann, Father Heilig had already determined to replace him. He learned the truth later and apologized, but he allowed the new appointments to

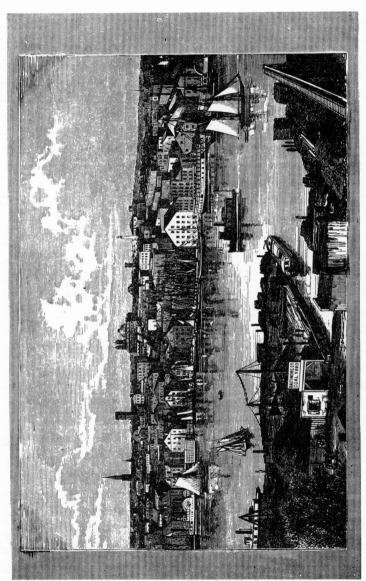

Baltimore: view from Federal Hill, about 1850

stand, and toward the end of 1848 Father Bernard Hafkenscheid arrived as the new Vice-Provincial of the American houses.

Considering the troubles in both Europe and America, it is amazing that John Neumann accomplished anything at all during the twenty-three months he ruled the ten Redemptorist houses and more than seventy missions in America, but he did. He placed the work of the Order on a more stable base, spiritually and materially. He strengthened observance of the Rule in all the houses and he selected a site in Cumberland, Maryland for the first Redemptorist house of studies in the United States. His greatest accomplishment, however, was in welcoming the School Sisters of Notre Dame to America, and helping them to establish themselves firmly in this country.

The sisters had arrived in the United States in the summer of 1847, with the intention of aiding the German colony at St. Mary's in Pennsylvania. St. Mary's was established in 1842 when a group of German families from Baltimore and Philadelphia had purchased about 35,000 acres of land in northwestern Pennsylvania, with the idea of forming there a purely German Catholic community. They worked hard, but the land they had purchased was unproductive and the whole scheme was impractical from the very beginning. The Redemptorists had become the spiritual directors of the community and, rather imprudently, had invested a good deal of their own money in the project. Without knowing too much about St. Mary's, King Ludwig of Bavaria had contributed substantial amounts of money to it, and it was through the Mission Society which he had founded that the School Sisters of Notre Dame were invited to come from Munich in 1847.

No one had bothered to ask permission, however, from Bishop O'Connor of Pittsburgh, in whose diocese the community was located, and when the sisters arrived, they were confronted not only with the dilapidated state of the colony but also with the fact that they had come without the bishop's approval. Bishop O'Connor finally consented to allow a few sisters to remain at St. Mary's, but it was clearly no place to establish their motherhouse in the United States. It was at this point that Father Neumann stepped in. He offered the sisters property owned by the Redemptorists in Baltimore on condition that they would teach in the school of St. Alphonsus. This they agreed to do, and a close association was formed between the Redemptorist Fathers and the School Sisters of Notre Dame which was to continue for many years.

Another group of sisters also benefited from Father Neumann's term as Superior. The Oblate Sisters of Providence were a congregation of black sisters which had been founded in 1828 in Baltimore. Their Order had not prospered, however, and in 1847 they were reduced to three members. At this point Archbishop Eccleston determined to suppress them, but Father Neumann persuaded him to change his mind and provided the sisters with Redemptorist directors and confessors. The Order revived, and today has many convents and schools in the United States and in other countries.

The new Vice-Provincial, Father Bernard Hafkenscheid, was a man large of mind and body. When he took office in January 1849, he appointed John Neumann as one of his consultors. The two became fast friends and Hafkenscheid called Neumann "my right arm."

These three years, 1849 through 1851, were relatively quiet and happy ones for Father Neumann. Relieved of the burdens of administration, he could devote himself to the parish work and teaching which he loved so much. He was confessor to several convents of nuns in Baltimore, including the Sisters of Charity at Mt. Hope Hospital, the School Sisters of Notre Dame and the Carmelites. One Carmelite nun was to say of him later: "Father Neumann contributed much to the perfection of our Sisters. His instructions and exhortations were animated by his own enthusiasm for the honor of God, the sublime end of the religious state. They inflamed our hearts with an ardent desire for religious perfection, for a total oblation to God."

The year 1850 saw the establishment of the American Redemptorists as an independent province of their own, and the founding of the seminary in Cumberland, Maryland. The Order was growing in America and beginning to lose its exclusively German character.

Another facet of Redemptorist life could begin to

be implemented about this time—the organization of trained bands of preachers to give parish missions. Among these early missioners were several young converts who would gain prominence in the history of the Church in America: Isaac Hecker, Clarence Walworth, Augustine Hewitt, George Deshon, a graduate of West Point and a classmate of Ulysses S. Grant, and Francis Baker, a former Episcopal minister. All five would later leave the Redemptorist Order to found the Paulists, but it is interesting to remember that they began their careers as spiritual brothers of John Neumann.

It was during these years also that Neumann was able to do a little more writing. He started a revision of his *Bible History*, and it is thought that he intended an English translation of his *Larger Catechism*, but unfortunately he never completed it. His papers from this time also included long notes on theology, enough for a full treatise, but this too was never published.

In January 1851 he was appointed rector of St. Alphonsus' Church in Baltimore, and he never again had time for extensive writing. Toward the end of 1851 Archbishop Eccleston died and was replaced by the former Bishop of Philadelphia, Francis Patrick Kenrick. The new archbishop, who had known Father Neumann slightly, now got to know him very well, and chose Neumann as his confessor. This friendship was to have serious consequences for John Neumann. Philadelphia was still without a bishop, and Archbishop Kenrick had been asked by Rome to recommend his successor.

9

Successor of the Apostles

PHILADELPHIA IN 1852 was a city of about four hundred thousand people. At the time of the American Revolution it had been the largest city in the colonies, and after London the second largest English-speaking city in the world, but early in the nineteenth century New York had surpassed it in population. William Penn's City of Brotherly Love had, however, preserved its reputation as a city of refinement and culture, and enjoyed its pre-eminence as the Birthplace of American Independence.

The Pennsylvania colony had not been as inimical to Catholics as had some of the other colonies, and there were in pre-Revolutionary Philadelphia two parishes: St. Joseph's, the first Catholic church in Pennsylvania, and St. Mary's, built some years later. In fact, by 1775 no other colony except Maryland had as many Catholics as did Pennsylvania, and at one point in the 1700s, St. Joseph's was the only place in the British dominions where Mass was publicly celebrated.

During the Revolution, Catholics gained a certain amount of acceptance they had not previously enjoyed in the colonies. Besides the fact that the percentage of Catholic soldiers in the American army was substantially higher than the percentage of Catholics in the population as a whole, the principal foreign support for the new Republic came from the two Catholic governments of France and Spain. Both nations had representatives accredited to the American government, and on several occasions members of Congress actually attended Mass in one of Philadelphia's Catholic churches, to the great dismay and disgust of some of the more rabidly anti-Catholic newspaper editors.

The climax occurred on May 8, 1780. The Spanish Minister, Don Juan de Miralles, had died, and Congress was invited to attend a special Requiem Mass at St. Joseph's. A few members refused, but most were present. Reporting the incident later, but still in a state of outrage and shock, the *Royal Gazette* of New York described what happened:

> When the procession arrived at the Roman Catholic chapel, the priest presented the holy water to M. Lucerne, who, after sprinkling himself, presented it to Mr. Huntington, the President of the Congress. The Calvinist paused a considerable time, near a minute, but at last his affection conquered all scruples of conscience, and he be-

sprinkled and sanctified himself with all the adroit-
ness of a veteran Catholic, when all his brethren of
the Congress, without hesitation, followed the
righteous example of their proselytized President.
Before the company, which was extremely num-
merous, left the chapel curiosity induced some
persons to uncover the bier, when they were highly
enraged at finding the whole thing a sham—there
being no corpse under the cloth—the body of the
Spanish gentleman having been interred at Morris-
town. The bier was surrounded by wax candles,
and every member of this egregious Congress, now
reconciled to the popish communion, carried a
taper in his hand.

By 1852, Philadelphia's Catholic population had
grown to about ninety thousand, most of them Irish
and German immigrants. The Diocese of Philadelphia
had been erected in 1808, when Baltimore was first
divided, and Pittsburgh had been taken from it in
1843, as we have seen, but in 1852 it still included the
eastern half of Pennsylvania, all of Delaware, and the
southern part of New Jersey—about thirty-five
thousand square miles, with a total Catholic
population of about 170,000. Today the same area
has seven dioceses and part of an eighth.

The new archbishop of Baltimore, Francis Patrick
Kenrick, had been a bishop in Philadelphia for twenty
years, first as coadjutor to Bishop Conwell and then
as ordinary of the diocese himself. His brother was
Archbishop Peter Kenrick of St. Louis. During his
term as Bishop of Philadelphia, Archbishop Kenrick
had seen the diocese expand tremendously. Besides

founding many new parishes, he had begun a
diocesan seminary, had invited several Orders of men
and women to come to Philadelphia, and had started
building a new cathedral, one of the most beautiful
and most imposing in America. The building projects
were expensive, however, and when he was
transferred to Baltimore, the diocese was still heavily
in debt. Archbishop Kenrick had a personal interest,
therefore, in recommending a successor who would
carry on and complete the work he had begun.

As Archbishop of Baltimore he was Metropolitan
of the province which included Philadelphia, and it
was his canonical duty to suggest names to Rome
from whom the new bishop would be selected.
Besides taking counsel with the bishops of his own
province, Archbishop Kenrick asked the advice of
other bishops as well, and as 1852 wore on, it seemed
that half the bishops in the United States had someone
to propose as the new Ordinary of Philadelphia.

There was one important factor to consider. There
were at this time about five million Germans living in
the United States. Many of them were Catholics, and
they felt that there should be more bishops of German
origin in the American hierarchy. They had made
their dissatisfaction known back in Germany and
Austria in no uncertain terms, and King Ludwig of
Bavaria, always interested in the condition of
German Catholics in America, had put pressure on
the Holy See to do something about the situation.

The result of King Ludwig's complaints was that
while Rome did not rush to appoint German bishops

Archbishop Francis Patrick Kenrick

for the United States, Cardinal Franzoni, speaking for Pope Pius ix, issued instructions that in dioceses which had a large foreign-speaking Catholic population, new bishops should be chosen from priests who had a good knowledge of the foreign language. Since Philadelphia was gaining more and more Germans yearly, Archbishop Kenrick felt that a German-speaking bishop was a necessity.

His choice fell ever more decidedly on his confessor, Father John Neumann, and he began proposing Neumann's name in letters to the other bishops. Agreement was not unanimous. One of the most vocal opponents was Neumann's own friend, Bishop O'Connor of Pittsburgh. Although he had publicly referred to John Neumann as a saint, Bishop O'Connor did not think Neumann was equipped to govern a diocese as large as Philadelphia. Some of the other bishops also had reservations. Several wondered whether Neumann's Bohemian ancestry would cause him to lose the respect of native Americans; others whether his English was good enough; others whether his appearance was imposing enough for a bishop; others whether his vow of poverty as a Redemptorist would interfere with his administration of the diocese.

Though he listened to all the objections and urged their authors to write to Rome themselves, Archbishop Kenrick persevered in his choice and included John Neumann's name among the three he forwarded to the Holy See.

While all these letters were circulating among the

American hierarchy, the subject of them was ignorant of what was happening. When John Neumann finally discovered what was in the air, he was thunderstruck. On his knees and with tears in his eyes, he begged Archbishop Kenrick to withdraw his name, but the Archbishop refused. Neumann persuaded the Provincial, Father Hafkenscheid, to write a letter to the Redemptorist superiors in Rome protesting the appointment. He had prayers said in his own church of St. Alphonsus, and asked all the convents of sisters he knew in Baltimore to pray for a special intention—that he might escape the office of bishop.

The final decision, however, now rested with the Holy Father. Pope Pius ix was one of the great popes of modern times. His thirty-two year reign spanned the middle of the nineteenth century, and is the longest in the history of the Church after that of St. Peter. Dozens of stories are told about Pius ix's wit and urbanity, but he was also a holy priest, and he could recognize holiness in others. On February 1, 1852 he made his choice, and named John Neumann to be the fourth bishop of Philadelphia. The Holy Father also knew his man well enough to add that Neumann must accept the appointment "under obedience and without appeal."

Archbishop Kenrick received official word of the appointment one month later, on March 1. He walked to St. Alphonsus' Rectory and asked for Father Neumann. Finding him out, the Archbishop went to Neumann's room, laid his own bishop's ring and pectoral cross on the table, and left. When Father

Neumann returned and discovered that it was Archbishop Kenrick who had left the ring and cross, the
meaning of the visit was clear. Neumann spent the
rest of the day and all that night on his knees in
prayer, but God had spoken through His Vicar and
there was nothing to do but accept.

Not all the bishops were enthusiastic about
Neumann's appointment, but all accepted the Holy
Father's decision. The consecration was set for
Passion Sunday, March 28, 1852 in St. Alphonsus'
Church in Baltimore. It was John Neumann's
forty-first birthday. He took as his motto the words:
Passio Christi, conforta me—"Passion of Christ,
strengthen me." Mindful of the terrible responsibility
being placed upon him, he confided to a fellow
Redemptorist on the eve of his consecration, "I would
rather die tomorrow than be consecrated bishop."

The consecration was performed by Archbishop
Kenrick, assisted by Bishop Bernard O'Reilly of Hart-
ford. Several other bishops were invited, but were
unable to attend. About twenty-five priests were
present, several of whom would later become bishops
themselves, and a great crowd of the Catholic
faithful. It was a gala day in Baltimore for everyone
except John Neumann. After the ceremony, attired
for the first time in his episcopal vestments, he said to
his Redemptorist brothers, "The Church treats her
bishops like a mother treats a child. When she wants
to place a burden on him, she gives him new clothes."

No one from Bishop Neumann's immediate family
was present at his consecration. His mother had died

three years before and his father and sisters were still living in Bohemia. The only one who might have been present, his brother Wenzel, was a Redemptorist lay-brother in Detroit. The Provincial, Father Hafkenscheid, had offered to let him come for the ceremony, but in his humility Wenzel had refused because the trip would be too expensive.

Bishop Neumann departed for Philadelphia on Tuesday, March 30, 1852. He had in his pocket a gift of six hundred dollars from the people of St. Alphonsus' parish and an additional five hundred dollars from the Redemptorist community—more than he had ever personally possessed in his whole life.

Though some of the priests and people in Philadelphia may have had reservations about their new bishop, the reception they gave him was warm and cordial. Father Edward Sourin, the administrator of the diocese, had suggested that instead of an expensive reception the bishop would be more pleased to have a new school established in the diocese, and so this was done. The bishop *was* pleased.

The preliminary greetings over, Bishop Neumann began the day after his arrival to become acquainted with his priests and people, and to visit the churches in the city. On one of his early visitations he stopped at the county jail where two brothers, Polish immigrants, were awaiting execution for murder. As a result of Bishop Neumann's visit the two brothers agreed to see a priest, and were reconciled to the Church before they died.

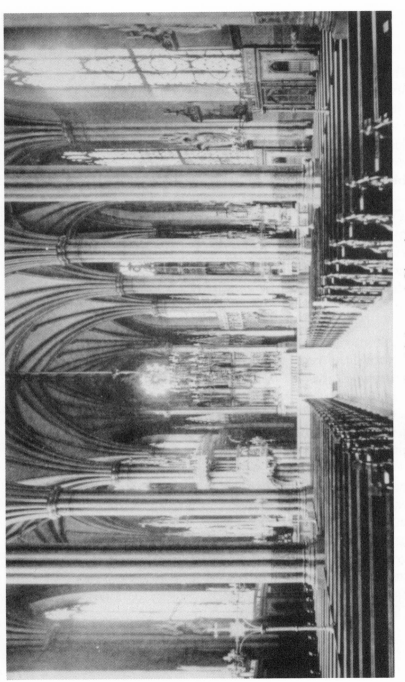

Baltimore: St. Alphonsus' Church
[where St. John Neumann was consecrated bishop]

Slightly over a month after he had arrived in Philadelphia, John Neumann was summoned back to Baltimore, in May 1852, to attend the first national council of the bishops of the United States. There had been provincial councils in Baltimore before, seven in fact, but this was the first Plenary Council of all the bishops and archbishops in the country. Today there are over three hundred bishops in the United States, but in 1852 there were thirty-one—six archbishops and twenty-five bishops. Two-thirds of them had been born in Europe. Most were relatively young men—only one was over sixty, and four were younger than John Neumann's forty-one years. Bishop Neumann was, of course, the only Redemptorist bishop, but there was also one Sulpician, two Dominicans, two Jesuits and two Vincentians.

The Council opened on May 9, 1852 with a procession from the archbishop's residence to Baltimore's Cathedral—the first time such an event was ever seen in the United States. In the ten days they were in session, the bishops discussed several important topics, including the problem of trusteeism, still plaguing the Church, and the need for parochial schools. Both of these items would be vital concerns of Bishop Neumann upon his return to Philadelphia.

The Council also recommended the establishment of eleven new dioceses, including one in Newark, New Jersey. Since this would draw territory from the Diocese of Philadelphia, this decision was also of concern to the new bishop. In addition, the Council adopted Bishop Neumann's *Larger Catechism* as the

official one for use in German parishes, and commis-
sioned him to write on behalf of the American hierarchy to the Leopoldine Foundation in Vienna,
thanking them for their support in the past, and
asking them to continue it in the future.

On his return from Baltimore Bishop Neumann
threw himself into the work of governing his diocese.
His daily schedule seems unbelievable, and we can
understand it only when we learn that in imitation of
St. Alphonsus, Neumann had made a vow never to
waste a minute of time.

He resumed the visitation of the parishes in his
diocese, and continued to address the Catholic
societies in Philadelphia. One lecture he gave to a
prominent Catholic literary group is worth remem-
bering. All pursuit of knowledge, the bishop said,
should be made to further the interests of God. Study
should begin with a prayer, and the fruits of reading
should be used in God's service. Sound, useful
knowledge, he continued, could come from perusing
only works which have truth in their pages. The false
ideas coming from certain philosophies in France and
Germany bring no increase in real learning. The
writings of the Transcendentalists, he declared, as
well as the publications of the so-called socialists,
have no place in any Catholic library. Reading the
romantic novels of the period, the bishop warned,
had a dangerous tendency, filling the mind with vain
imagery and displacing the hallowed love of God
with the unhallowed love of His creatures. Giving a
practical rule for the value of reading, the bishop said

that in his opinion if one could not recite a fervent and heartfelt Lord's Prayer after persuing a book, he could be sure the reading had done damage to his soul.

Quite a strong sermon from the Gentle Bishop, as Archbishop Kenrick called him, and certainly more than the good people of the literary society had bargained for!

Almost as soon as he arrived in Philadelphia, Bishop Neumann set to work on a project which he considered to be the most important in his diocese: the establishment of a system of Catholic schools. During the 1830s and 1840s the public school system in the United States had undergone profound changes. Standards were raised and organization introduced, but religious teaching had been virtually eliminated. If the Catholic Church was mentioned at all, it was often in ridicule, and the American bishops realized that the whole system of public instruction as then constituted was a serious threat to the faith of Catholic children. After trying unsuccessfully to obtain public funds for separate Catholic schools, the bishops were forced to undertake the enormous burden of trying to provide private parochial schools for their people.

As an active pastor and confessor, Bishop Neumann had been aware of the danger of the public school system for many years. In 1841, in a letter to the Archbishop of Vienna, he had written a strong indictment of a system which left religion out of the education of Catholic children. He had declared that while parents were permitted to rear their children in whatever religion they chose, this apparent liberality was harmful, particularly when a teacher's attitude might instill in a child a feeling of indifference toward religion. Even the textbooks were often far from unprejudiced, and some of them contained malicious perversions of truth together with the grossest lies against the doctrines and practices of the Catholic Church. These circumstances combined to threaten the spiritual ruin of Catholic children.

As bishop, therefore, John Neumann had wholeheartedly endorsed the exhortation of the Plenary Council of Baltimore to the faithful:

Give your children a Christian education, that is, an education based on religious principles, accompanied by religious practices and always subordinate to religious influence. Be not led astray by the false and delusive theories which are so prevalent, and which leave youth without religion, and, consequently, without anything to control the passions, promote the real happiness of the individual, and make society find in the increase of its members, a source of security and prosperity. Listen not to those who would persuade you that religion can be separated from secular instruction. If your children, while they advance in human sciences , are not taught the science of the saints, their minds will be filled with every error, their hearts will be receptacles of every vice. . . . Encourage the establishment and support of Catholic schools; make every sacrifice which will be necessary for this object.

To implement this program, one of Bishop Neumann's first actions was to set up a central board of education in the diocese. Besides the bishop, the board would consist of the pastor and two laymen from each parish, and would have general supervision of the school-building program throughout the diocese. The board could recommend a general plan of instruction, and had some authority over the distribution of funds, but the hiring of teachers and the paying of salaries were left to the pastor. Here was the general outline for the parochial school system eventually adopted in the United States, and it stands as one of Bishop Neumann's most important achievements.

In response to John Neumann's unrelenting efforts, the number of parochial schools increased rapidly in Philadelphia. When he arrived as bishop, there were about five hundred children in Catholic schools throughout the diocese. Eighteen months later there were five thousand. One year after that, nine thousand. So strong were the foundations that Bishop Neumann laid, and so lasting their effects, that in 1963 Cardinal Krol of Philadelphia could remark that while Philadelphia was eighth in the country in total Catholic population, it was first in the total number of students in Catholic educational institutions.

Whatever may be the future of Catholic schools in the United States, and no one can deny that they have come upon hard times in recent years, it is significant that our two new saints, Elizabeth Seton and John Neumann, were both intimately connected with the formation of the Catholic school system in America. Perhaps there is a lesson here, and a message for all of us.

Besides the program of building schools, Bishop Neumann was also faced with the necessity of building more and more new parishes. Here he had to contend with the same dilemma all the American bishops faced—whether to expand and keep expanding to take care of the flood of new immigrants, even in the face of astronomical debts, or to hold back until expenses could be met, and thereby run the risk of losing many souls from the Church for want of proper facilities to care for them. As did most of the American bishops, Bishop Neumann chose the former course, relying on the Providence of God and the generosity of his people. He went ahead building schools and churches as they were needed. In his first thirty-four months as bishop he completed six churches begun by Archbishop Kenrick, rebuilt six more, and added thirty new ones to his diocese—an average of more than one a month.

Visitation of his diocese was another project close to Bishop Neumann's heart. The Council of Trent had prescribed that a bishop should visit every parish in his diocese at least once every two years. This rule had been made with the small dioceses of Europe in mind, not one like Philadelphia with its thirty-five thousand square miles, much of it in rugged, mountain country. Bishop Neumann was determined to fulfill the ordinance of Trent, however, if he possibly could, and in so doing he endeared himself to

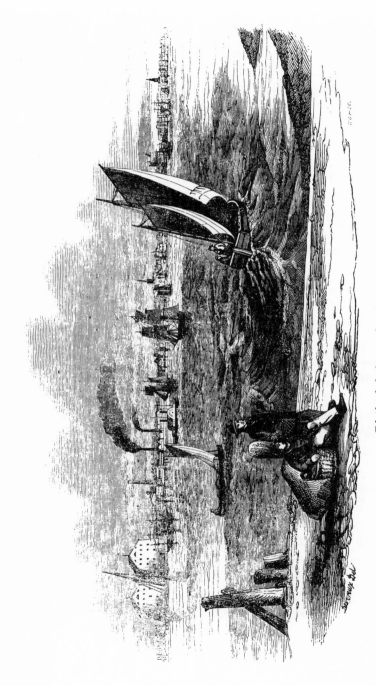

Philadelphia, about 1852

his scattered flock. He used all sorts of transportation, both ancient and modern, including the most ancient of all—his own feet. Sometimes he would be away only a day or two; other times he spent as long as seven weeks visiting the mountain parishes of his diocese.

His visitations were not only administrative but spiritual as well. Besides examining the parish registers and financial accounts, he would hear confessions, preach in English and German, administer Confirmation and visit the sick. He often carried a portable altar with him to the homes of the infirm, where he would say Mass and confirm. When he found a small community which had a few Catholics but no church, he would choose some definite house where the people could gather on Sunday to say the rosary and other prayers. He often had to confirm in buildings other than churches where no churches were available—schools, private homes, public halls and even court houses. Bishop Neumann always loved these visitations and the contact they gave him with the simple people of his diocese, and no difficulties of weather or terrain ever deterred him from his journeys.

Throughout his life, John Neumann's great devotions were to Our Lord in the Blessed Sacrament and to our Blessed Lady, and he was always eager to inculcate these devotions into his people. To increase love for the Blessed Sacrament in his diocese, he introduced the practice of the Forty Hours on a regular schedule. The Forty Hours' Devotion com-

memorates the time between Our Lord's death on the
Cross and His Resurrection on Easter Sunday, traditionally a period which lasted forty hours. Throughout a continuous span of forty hours the Blessed
Sacrament is exposed on the altar for public
veneration, and the faithful are encouraged to visit
Our Lord, taking turns so that the church is never left
empty. The devotion had been practiced in individual
churches in the United States before Bishop
Neumann, but he was the first bishop to set it up on
an organized, diocesan schedule. Several of his priests
advised against it, however, fearing that it would
expose the Blessed Sacrament to possible profanation.
Bishop Neumann turned the problem over in his mind
for a long time, and was finally convinced that the
decision he reached was in accordance with God's
will.

The 1840s, as we have seen, were the years of the
first great surge of immigrants into the United States.
The fact that there were so many of them, that they
were foreigners, and that a good proportion were also
Catholics, were all items calculated to arouse the hostility of the native Americans. Boston, New York,
Philadelphia and other cities had all had anti-Catholic
riots, and had seen Catholic convents and churches
burned to the ground. Philadelphia had had two
churches burned before John Neumann became
bishop, and so the fear of further outbreaks and
outrage was not entirely without foundation. While
pondering this problem one night in connection with
the Forty Hours' Devotion, Bishop Neumann fell

asleep at his desk. When he awoke, the candle he was using had burned down and charred some of his papers, but had not set them afire. He knelt down to thank God that nothing more serious had happened, and he seemed to hear the voice of Our Lord speaking to him: "As the flames are burning here without consuming or injuring the writing, so shall I pour out my Grace in the Blessed Sacrament without prejudice to my honor. Fear no profanation, therefore, and hesitate no longer to carry out your design for my glory."

Believing this to be an authentic sign from God, Bishop Neumann established the devotion of the Forty Hours in April 1853, beginning in the church of St. Philip Neri, who had been the one to introduce the devotion in Rome. The Forty Hours' Devotion spread to other dioceses, and eventually came to be practiced throughout the United States.

While he could rejoice in the spiritual and material growth of his diocese during his first years as bishop, John Neumann had his share of troubles also. One of the most difficult and trying problems he had to face was that of church trustees, often made more difficult when the trustees were German. The Germans can be a very stubborn people, and when they get hold of an idea, they sometimes find it difficult to let go. Not all, to be sure, but a few of the Germans were determined to have their own churches run the way they wanted them run, and no bishop, Irish or German, was going to tell them otherwise.

In one small town, where a new church was being built, the German parishioners insisted that it should

St. John Neumann's bishop's ring and pectoral cross

be German- instead of English-speaking. Bishop
Neumann decided that the church should be
English-speaking, but that everyone in the parish
should join forces to build a German church as soon
as possible. Not content with this, and irate at the
bishop's decision, a few of the German hotheads
actually placed a railroad tie on the tracks to derail
his train as he left town. Fortunately the tie was de-
tected and the train stopped in time, but the perpetra-
tors followed Bishop Neumann to Philadelphia and
stood outside his house shouting insults. The bishop
was actually forced to excommunicate them before
they returned to their senses and asked his pardon.

A more serious situation arose in the German
parish in South Philadelphia, Holy Trinity. Archbishop Kenrick, when he was Bishop of Philadelphia,
had had a running feud for more than ten years with
the trustees of Holy Trinity over the administration of
church property. In 1850 he proposed to settle the
problem by petitioning the legislature to change the
church's charter to allow him to appoint the trustees.
Tired of quarreling, many of the trustees agreed, but
a small faction would not yield and actually broke up
a meeting the bishop had called to discuss the matter.
In exasperation, Archbishop Kenrick excommuni-
cated the ringleaders and placed the church under
interdict, which meant that Mass could not be said
there nor the sacraments administered. Archbishop
Kenrick made one more attempt to settle the question
by offering the church to the Jesuits, but the recalcitrant trustees obtained an injunction in court, and the

interdict was renewed.

Thus matters stood when Bishop Neumann arrived in 1852. With Holy Trinity closed, the German Catholics of South Philadelphia were without a church of their own, and were rapidly becoming demoralized. Bishop Neumann realized, however, that an important principle was at stake. He informed the rebellious trustees that if they wished to have the interdict lifted, they must cede the church property over to him as bishop. In reply they renewed their petition in court and actually won a decision giving them title to the church. The bishop had no recourse but to order construction to begin on a new German parish in South Philadelphia, St. Alphonsus. Meanwhile he appealed the decision of the lower courts to the Supreme Court of Pennsylvania.

The case dragged on in court for almost two years, while the bishop was treated to a torrent of abuse, both oral and written, from the disobedient trustees. The final hearing took place in March 1854, in the Supreme Court chamber, before Judge George Woodward. The trustees were represented by a prominent non-Catholic lawyer, and the judge himself was not a Catholic. Bishop Neumann appeared to give evidence in his own cause.

"Tell me," asked the judge, "why you call your church Roman Catholic."

"Our church is called Roman Catholic," replied Bishop Neumann, "because the Pope who is its head resides in Rome. According to the laws of the Pope the bishops administer their dioceses, and according to the laws of the bishops the pastors govern their congregations. If anyone wants to be a member of our Catholic Church he must be united through the pastor with the bishop and through the bishop with the Pope. The union is affected through spiritual obedience. Whoever does not render this obedience does not belong to the Catholic Church, because this arrangement is its essential, its unchangeable constitution."

The judge asked the rebellious trustees if this were true.

"Yes," they replied.

Judge Woodward then delivered his decision: "You Germans are a disgrace to our city. For ninety years you have been quarreling with your bishop." (Actually this was somewhat of an exaggeration, because the United States had had bishops for only about sixty-five years, but the point about the quarreling was true enough.) The judge continued: "You had an Irishman for bishop, an American, and now you have a German. You are satisfied with none, obedient to none. If you want to be Catholics you must obey the Pope and the bishops in all ecclesiastical affairs. You cannot expect that the court will protect your disobedience."

The lawyer for the trustees replied that the bishop was a secret Jesuit and that the Jesuits were trying to accumulate for themselves all the wealth of the world. Judge Woodward disposed of this argument in a few words.

"If the Jesuits come, and in a legal manner acquire

the whole city of Philadelphia, our laws will protect them. If the Germans are not satisfied with their bishop, they can give up their faith anytime. There is freedom of religion with us, but as long as they are Catholics they must obey the Pope and the bishops in all religious matters."

Bishop Neumann had won his case, and he recovered legal title to Holy Trinity Church. Within a short time loyal trustees were elected and the interdict lifted. Five years later the parish charter was amended to allow the bishop to name the trustees. The Bishop of Philadelphia had gained an important decision for the Church in America and a crucial victory in the battle against trusteeism.

There was one other serious problem facing Bishop Neumann upon his arrival in Philadelphia—the continuation of the new Cathedral of Sts. Peter and Paul, begun by Archbishop Kenrick. When the new bishop arrived, the rear wall and two side walls of the Cathedral were standing, but the available money had been used up. Bishop Neumann was willing to incur new debts for the diocese in order to build churches and schools where none existed before, but he felt the diocese could get along for a while with the Pro-Cathedral of St. John, and he insisted that no construction be done on the new Cathedral until funds were available. There was criticism from some of the priests and laity, but the bishop was adamant, and so work on the new Cathedral proceeded slowly.

Thus matters stood as the summer of 1854 drew to a close. In the two and one-half years that he had been Bishop of Philadelphia, John Neumann's untiring labors had brought great benefits, both spiritual and material, to his flock. But now there would be a temporary change. Pope Pius ix had announced that he would define the Immaculate Conception of the Blessed Virgin Mary as a dogma of the Catholic Faith, and he invited all the bishops of the world who could attend to be present in Rome on December 8. The wish of the Holy Father, and his own devotion to our Blessed Mother, urged Bishop Neumann to make the trip. He could take the opportunity to make his official *ad limina* visit to Rome, required of bishops every five years. The trip would also give him a chance to visit his family in Bohemia, whom he had not seen for eighteen years. He accepted the Holy Father's invitation, and prepared to leave for Rome in October 1854.

10

Rome and Bohemia

1854 WAS A STORMY YEAR ON THE ATLANTIC, but even so Bishop Neumann's return trip to Europe was faster and more pleasant than the one he had made in 1836. Seventeen days after leaving New York he landed in Le Havre, the same port from which he had departed eighteen years previously. Traveling on to Paris, he wired his father in Bohemia that he would visit him as soon as his business in Rome was completed. The old man was of course delighted, but with the candor permitted the very old and the very young, he is said to have remarked, "Why do they have to bring American bishops to Rome to tell us that the most holy Virgin was conceived without sin when we have always believed it here?"

Leaving Paris and moving south to Marseilles, Bishop Neumann embarked on a small Mediterranean steamer for Civita Vecchia, the port of Rome. On board he met an American lady, Mrs. Sara Peters, who had been interested in the Catholic Faith for some time but had done nothing about it. She declared later that her conversation with Bishop Neumann was the turning point in her life, and shortly afterwards entered the Catholic Church.

Bishop Neumann arrived in Rome in November, the first time in his life he had ever seen the Eternal City. He remained there for two months, living with his fellow Redemptorists and insisting that he be treated no differently from any of the other fathers. He dressed in the Redemptorist habit, and in his walks about the city refused to wear any distinguishing mark to indicate that he was a bishop.

One of his favorite devotions was making the pilgrimage on foot to the Seven Churches of Rome, usually not breaking his fast until he had completed the journey. The seven great basilicas of Rome are not close together, as any one knows who has visited them, and a pilgrimage on foot will take the better part of a full day. To accomplish it while fasting is even more arduous, but Bishop Neumann is said to have made the pilgrimage at least five or six times during his stay in Rome.

Not for centuries had Rome witnessed an event as moving and as colorful as the Definition of the Immaculate Conception of the Blessed Virgin by Pope Pius ix on December 8, 1854. Fifty-three cardinals, one hundred and forty bishops and more than fifty thousand priests, religious and laymen crowded St. Peter's Basilica. As the Holy Father uttered the actual

Pope Pius IX

words of the Definition, tears were streaming down his face:

> We declare, pronounce and define that the doctrine which holds that the Blessed Virgin Mary in the first moment of her conception, by the singular grace and privilege of Almighty God, in view of the merits of Jesus Christ, the Savior of the human race, was preserved immune from all stain of original guilt, has been revealed by God and therefore must be firmly and constantly believed by all the faithful.

That night all Rome was ablaze with lights to honor the Immaculate Mother. To his people in Philadelphia, Bishop Neumann wrote of this great event:

> To have been present on so glorious an occasion, to have taken part therein as chief pastor of the Diocese of Philadelphia and one of the representatives of the Church in America, is an honor and happiness which my words cannot describe, but for which I return and forever will return humble thanks to Our Lord Jesus Christ.

On December 16 he presented his report on the state of his diocese to the Roman officials. No one could fail to be impressed by what he had accomplished in less than three years as Bishop of Philadelphia, and no one was more pleased with the report than the Holy Father himself. He received the bishop in audience and remarked, "Bishop Neumann of Philadelphia, isn't obedience better than sacrifice?" an allusion to the fact that he had had to command John Neumann to accept the office of bishop.

Leaving Rome late in December, Bishop Neumann traveled north toward Austria and Bohemia to visit his family. He stayed whenever possible at Redemptorist houses, and traveled dressed like an ordinary priest, but nevertheless his reputation preceded him. There is an interesting story told about his trip. He had gathered together in Rome and at other shrines a large packet of relics and religious articles which he intended to take back with him to Philadelphia. Somewhere along the way the packet was lost, and he spent many hours telegraphing back along the route inquiring about it, but without success. Finally he had recourse to the saint most Catholics pray to when they have lost something. He promised if the package were found to say Mass in St. Anthony's honor, and to promote special devotion to him in one of the churches of his diocese. Hardly had he finished his prayer when a young man stepped up to him and said, "Bishop, here is your lost package." Overjoyed at having his relics returned, the bishop turned to thank the young man, but the latter was nowhere to be seen. Needless to say, the promise to honor St. Anthony was kept.

By the time he left Vienna and arrived in Prague, it was impossible for Bishop Neumann to continue his journey in secret. He was invited to dine with the former Emperor Ferdinand, who had abdicated six years previously in favor of his nephew, Franz Josef. After visiting the motherhouse of the Sisters of St. Charles, where his own sister, Joan, was Mother Superior, John Neumann arrived on January 30 in Budweis. He hoped to reach his native village of

Prachatitz seen from the air

Prachatitz quietly at night, but his former neighbors had no intention of letting this happen. Small boys were sent out ahead as couriers to advise the town of the bishop's progress, and as he rode along in a sleigh, people came out of their homes to kneel in the snow for his blessing.

When he arrived in Nettolitz, the next village to Prachatitz, the whole town had turned out, and he was literally forced to remain there for the night. Still trying to avoid publicity, Bishop Neumann suggested to his young nephew, John Berger, the son of his sister Catherine, that they leave early in the morning and walk the few miles to Prachatitz by the back road. But this was not to be. As the bishop and his nephew emerged from the parish rectory in the morning, a sleigh was already waiting for them—not the simple one in which they had arrived the day before, but the personal sleigh of Prince Schwarzenberg, with four horses and a liveried coachman. The bishop had no recourse but to surrender, and to accept the accolades of his former neighbors. The young couriers had done their work well, and as Bishop Neumann neared his native village, bells were ringing, a band was playing, guns were being fired and the whole town was on hand to give him a royal welcome. Almost nineteen years to the day after he had left home, he was reunited with his father and his youngest sister, Louise.

Bishop Neumann stayed seven days in Prachatitz and in leaving he was finally able to win at least one round in his battle against notoriety. He slipped out at daybreak one morning, and avoided the bands and bells that were prepared for him. A few more visits, including the Cistercians at Hohenfurt who had been his teachers so many years before, and John Neumann was on his way back to America. Together with Archbishop John Hughes of New York, he left Liverpool early in March and arrived in New York on his birthday, March 28, 1855. In leaving the United States and returning to it, Bishop Neumann provided evidence which would one day solve a scholars' problem about him. Records were kept somewhat haphazardly in the mid-nineteenth century, and while it was assumed that John Neumann had indeed become an American citizen, no formal statement of the fact could be found until someone thought to check the customs declaration he had filled out on re-entering the United States. In it he affirmed that he had been an American citizen since February 1848, and intended to remain one.

Archbishop Hughes (he had been named the first archbishop of New York in 1850) also filled out the customs form the same day, but declared that he was a subject of Great Britain (meaning Ireland, of course) and intended to remain one—a surprising and rather amusing admission from the man who had become known as the outspoken defender of the rights of American Catholics in the face of native bigotry.

As he stepped ashore once again in New York, John Neumann could remember the twenty-three weeks he had been away from Philadelphia as busy but happy ones. Now he must plunge again into his problems and duties as bishop of one of the largest and fastest-growing dioceses in the United States.

11

Tried in the Furnace

BISHOP NEUMANN RETURNED FROM ROME to Philadelphia at a time when a new wave of anti-Catholic feeling was reaching a climax in the United States. Some native Americans still shudder d at the thought that so many immigrants were l.   g in their country, but conditions were made worse by the arrival in the 1850s of small groups of violent radicals, mostly German and Italian, exiled from Europe after the revolutions of 1848. Denouncing the Catholic governments that had expelled them, these men entered a hot situation and helped it to boil over.

When Archbishop Gaetano Bedini, for example, stopped in the United States on his way to Brazil to assume his duties as Apostolic Nuncio, he was attacked by a violent mob and barely escaped with his life. The famous Jesuit missionary, Father John Bapst, was tarred and feathered in Maine, and Massachusetts passed a bigoted convent-inspection law. Catholics were attacked by another mob in Louisville, Kentucky, which burned their homes and left over twenty persons dead.

No mob scenes occurred in Philadelphia, but Bishop Neumann was treated to trouble of a more serious kind. The anti-Catholic forces had formed themselves into a political party, popularly known as the "Know-Nothings" because when questioned about their activities the members were instructed to say, "I do not know," or, "I know nothing." By 1854 they held the balance of power in the Pennsylvania legislature and were pushing for anti-Catholic laws. They found ready support among the few groups of disaffected parish trustees still remaining, and in 1855 they managed to enact a law preventing the bishops from transmitting any church property to their successors, and requiring that the control of all such property be in the hands of lay members of the congregation. A similar bill was also passed in New York. Actually only one or two parishes took advantage of the law to reject the authority of their bishop, but the whole problem of church property was a thorn in the sides of the American bishops for the next few years.

Bishop Neumann continued, nevertheless, to build the churches and schools which were so dear to his heart. A new orphanage was begun, primarily for German-speaking children, and a new congregation of sisters was founded, following the Rule of the Third Order of St. Francis. The times were hard, however, and some of Bishop Neumann's building projects suffered from lack of funds—especially the Cathedral, whose construction was proceeding much more slowly than he would have wished.

On a more personal note, Bishop Neumann's young nephew, John Berger, arrived from Europe in 1857 to study for the priesthood. He eventually followed his uncle in entering the Redemptorist Order, and became John Neumann's first and most important biographer, especially for the saint's early years.

One of the most severe trials Bishop Neumann had to undergo during this period of his life came to the surface shortly after his return from Rome, but it had been a source of anxiety to him from the time he became Bishop of Philadelphia. He knew that he was not popular with certain of the wealthier, more sophisticated Catholics of the city, both clergy and laity, who hoped to have in their bishop a social as well as a religious leader. Being of a quiet and retiring disposition, Bishop Neumann was not the socializing type. He would never willingly offend any of the more prominent members of his flock, but neither would he go out of his way to cultivate them. Snobbery or artificiality of any kind were totally foreign to John Neumann's nature, and though he genuinely sought to be a father to all his people, he was incapable of pretending to be what he was not. In reality he probably did feel more at home with the poor, especially the immigrants.   He had been a poor immigrant himself only a few years before, and he understood the bewilderment and turmoil which often afflicted the souls of these new arrivals.

*Philadelphia: Cathedral of Sts. Peter and Paul
under construction*

The number of poor Catholics, of course, far exceeded the number of rich ones in the Diocese of Philadelphia, but the latter were more eloquent, and were able to make their opinions known even as far away as Rome: Bishop Neumann did not cut the imposing figure one might reasonably expect to see in the bishop of the most cultured city in America; he seemed not to have a sure grasp of financial matters; his building program, especially school building, was sinking the diocese deeper and deeper into debt; his insistence on visiting personally all the outlying districts of his huge diocese meant that he was away from the city a good part of the time, and not available for consultation on more important matters; finally, the new Cathedral, the one building project which the bishop ought to have been promoting vigorously, was hardly moving at all, and Bishop Kenrick's dream had become an eyesore to the city rather than a landmark.

Though he refrained from answering these criticisms publicly, Bishop Neumann was well aware of them. They pained him deeply, not because of the personal affront to himself, but because they were a source of friction and alienation between him and his people.

Shortly after his return from Europe, therefore, in the spring of 1855, he determined to act. Archbishop Kenrick summoned the bishops of his district to meet in a provincial council at Baltimore in May, not a council of all the bishops of the United States, but only those under Kenrick's jurisdiction. It was here

that Bishop Neumann made a startling proposal. A
short time previously the Diocese of New York had
been divided. Newark was now separate, and also
Brooklyn. This made Philadelphia the largest diocese
in the United States both in area and in population.
Bishop Neumann proposed therefore that it was time
to consider dividing his diocese. Even though the
southern part of New Jersey had been given to the
Diocese of Newark, he still had twenty-nine thousand
square miles of territory to administer. He suggested
that the Diocese of Philadelphia be split and that a
new diocese be erected in Pottsville, Pennsylvania.

Though Pottsville never developed into a large
city, it seemed at the time to be centrally located, and
therefore Bishop Neumann's suggestion was not entirely without merit. What did amaze the bishops,
however, was Bishop Neumann's second suggestion:
that he be allowed to resign from Philadelphia and
take over the new diocese in Pottsville. If this were
not practical, he offered to accept either Wilmington,
North Carolina, or the Vicariate of Florida, two other
areas then under consideration to become dioceses.

In a long letter, two weeks after the council ended,
to Cardinal Franzoni in Rome, Bishop Neumann repeated his suggestion. After describing the size of his
diocese and the advantages of Pottsville as a new see,
he continued:

> As for myself, day and night I am filled with un-
> easiness and perpetual fear. The debts left me by
> my venerable predecessor cause me much anxiety.
> Because of circumstances here, a man of sharp in-

sight, brave and accustomed to direct temporal affairs is required. I, however, am timid, always hesitating, and possess a horror of business and pecuniary transactions.

To be sure, I am aware that all care regarding temporal things should be cast upon the Lord Who hath a care for us. My faith is weak, however, and the sins and negligences by which I have offended the good God strike fear into me, lest God abandon me and the faithful committed to my care. The City of Philadelphia, which has more than five hundred thousand inhabitants and (if you will pardon the statement) a very worldly character, needs someone else instead of myself who am too plain and not sufficiently talented; besides I love solitude. Since there is a proposal to erect many new dioceses, I thought it my duty to inform Your Eminence that I am most willing to be transferred to another see where a less gifted man would be required. For more than fifteen years I was occupied on the North American missions; I have loved corporal labors and journeys in the mountains and through the forests. Visiting Catholic families seperated from one another by long distances and preaching to them, etc. has been my greatest pleasure. The Vicariate of Florida, the Diocese of Wilmington in the State of North Carolina will be very poor and most laborious fields, and it will not be easy to find priests to take up the episcopal burden there. Because of my character, however, a great field of this kind would be most pleasing to me, provided the Holy Father, according to the light which God gives him, would declare it to be the Will of God.

In 1921, in declaring John Neumann's virtues to
have been heroic, Pope Benedict xv asserted: "This
offer of Bishop Neumann to leave Philadelphia was
positive proof of his magnanimity of soul."

In 1855, however, not everyone would have
agreed. Archbishop Kenrick urged his friend not to
leave Philadelphia, but Bishop O'Connor of
Pittsburgh took up the suggestion with an enthusiasm
which seemed at times embarrassing. Bishop
O'Connor was not Bishop Neumann's enemy. As we
have seen, he had known him in Pittsburgh, and
considered him to be a saint. Nor does it seem likely
that Bishop O'Connor hoped to be transferred to
Philadelphia himself. His name was never mentioned
as a possible successor to Bishop Neumann, and there
is no evidence that he ever sought the office. He
eventually resigned from his own See of Pittsburgh,
and spent the last years of his life as a Jesuit in Maryland. Bishop O'Connor was, however, impetuous,
and given to quick decisions which he did not then
easily abandon. He seems to have been honestly convinced that Bishop Neumann was not the man for
Philadelphia, and he said so often, and in no
uncertain terms.

The officials in Rome, however, in accordance with
their reputation for moving slowly, refused to be
swept into any hasty decisions. Pope Pius ix himself
had been impressed with Bishop Neumann's report on
the state of his diocese, and the pope was not easily
swayed by Bishop Neumann's low opinion of himself.
Archbishop Kenrick sent his own assessment of the

situation to Rome in an opinion filled with prudence
and good sense:

> The Bishop of Philadelphia has made known to
> me that he has written to the Holy See asking to be
> transferred elsewhere because of a lack of skill in
> finances and other matters. It seems to me that he
> should by all means be retained in the See of
> Philadelphia since he is a shining light because of
> his piety and his labors. I, indeed, confess that he is
> wanting a little in managing affairs, but I believe
> that he can appoint a vicar general, consultors and
> helpers, whose assistance will enable him to clear
> the debts and to smooth out matters. He is beloved
> by the clergy and people, although certain ones
> would like to see more urbane and polished
> manners.

As news of these deliberations spread, rumors
began to fly. Whatever deficiencies Bishop Neumann
may have had in administering his diocese were soon
magnified out of all proportion. Even some of the
bishops who were friendly to him, including Archbishop Kenrick himself for a time, wavered in their
loyalty as a result of the exaggerated stories ema-
nating from Philadelphia. A few discontented priests,
emboldened by all the criticism, even went so far as to
attack the bishop publicly at a synod of priests.
Bishop Neumann's imperturbable humility carried the
day, however, and the offenders later apologized.

With all the rumors and counter-rumors it is not
surprising that some bishops did feel that it would be
better for Bishop Neumann to resign from
Philadelphia, but one strong dissenting voice was

Philadelphia, about 1856

raised. "It will be a sad day for the Diocese of Philadelphia," said Bishop Fitzpatrick of Boston, "when it
shall lose him."

In reality, Bishop Neumann had never suggested
that he should resign completely as a bishop. Though
he certainly had never sought the episcopate, he had
accepted it at the express command of the pope, and
he therefore firmly believed that it was God's will for
him to serve the Church as bishop. He had
recommended only that he leave Philadelphia and
move to a smaller, less developed diocese, more
suited, as he thought, to his talents as a missionary.

The case dragged on in Rome for a year and a half,
and it was not until the end of 1856 that a decision
was finally given. In the meantime Bishop Neumann
continued to work for the salvation of souls and for
the good of his diocese. That he was afflicted by fears
of his own unworthiness no one can deny, but he
never gave any outward indication of his feelings,
and never used his episcopal authority to silence those
under his jurisdiction. His vow never to waste a
moment of time did not include defending himself
against his calumniators.

There were churches and schools to be dedicated,
instructions to be given, and visitations to be made
throughout his diocese. Four more religious orders
entered Philadelphia during this period to begin work
which would bear much fruit as the years went by:
the Holy Cross Sisters, the Holy Cross Brothers, the
Sisters of Notre Dame de Namur and the Christian
Brothers.

There were also sorrows which afflicted his people, and which affected the bishop more deeply than any of his personal problems. In July 1856, the people of St. Michael's parish hired a special train to take them to the country for a picnic. There was a delay in starting, the signals were not properly sent ahead, and the special train crashed head-on into another train coming in the opposite direction. Sixty-five people were killed and hundreds more injured, many of them children from St. Michael's School. Bishop Neumann did all that he could, visiting the hospitals himself, consoling, encouraging and administering the sacraments, but the tragedy was a great weight upon his soul

On a happier note, there occured during this period an incident which has become one of the most famous in Bishop Neumann's life, though he, in all likelihood, did not consider it so at the time. Among the Irish immigrants who came to America during the nineteenth century, there were a good many from the west of Ireland for whom Irish was still their native language. You may sometimes see the Irish language called *Gaelic*, especially in older books, but linguists now generally prefer the term *Gaelic* for the speech of Scotland, and *Irish* for that of Ireland; the two languages are closely related. Whichever name you prefer, there were native speakers of that language under Bishop Neumann's jurisdiction, and they knew no other tongue. He met some of these Irish immigrants on a visit to a remote part of his diocese, but was unable to converse with them. On his next visit, however, he had mastered enough of the language to be able to hear their confessions. The story goes that one old lady is said to have remarked, "Thanks be to God, we have an Irish Bishop." The Irish, never people to be outdone in generosity, responded to the bishop's kindness by making the story famous. It is now commemorated in one of the stained-glass windows in Bishop Neumann's Shrine in Philadelphia.

At last, on December 9, 1856, Rome reached a decision regarding the Diocese of Philadelphia and its bishop. Since the United States was at the time still technically a mission territory as far as the Church was concerned (the status was not officially changed until 1908), all American ecclesiastical affairs were handled in Rome by the Sacred Congregation *de Propaganda Fide*, shortened in typical American fashion to "the Propaganda." In our day the word *propaganda* has acquired a rather unpleasant connotation, but the Latin word from which it comes means simply "to spread" or "propagate." The Sacred Congregation *de Propaganda Fide* is, therefore, the office of the Roman Curia charged "with spreading the Faith," specifically with the supervision of the Church's missionary activity throughout the world. In countries or areas where there are very few Catholics, or where the resources of the Church are limited, all ecclesiastical business with Rome was, and to a great extent still is, handled through the Congregation *de Propaganda Fide*.

This arrangement is intended to be temporary—as

soon as the Church is sufficiently established so that
the country or area in question is no longer considered to be "mission territory," ecclesiastical jurisdiction is taken from the Propaganda, and divided
among the other congregations according to the
nature of the business to be transacted.

This "coming of age" for the Church in America
took place in 1908, as we have said, but in 1856
everything, including the division of dioceses and the
appointment of new bishops, was still administered
by the Propaganda.

The decision reached on December 9, duly ratified
by Pope Pius ix, adopted a suggestion made some
months before by Archbishop Kenrick. The Propaganda communicated its decision to the Archbishop
in February, and he received it on March 30, 1857.
Perhaps in deference to the Bishop of Philadelphia's
well-known humility, he himself was not consulted in
the matter, and first learned of Rome's decision in the
secular newspapers. Bishop Neumann was not to be
transferred to another diocese, but was to remain as
Bishop of Philadelphia. He was, however, to have an
assistant, a coadjutor, another bishop who would
help him in administering the affairs of the diocese.
The man named as the new coadjutor was a priest of
the Diocese of Cincinnati, James Frederick Wood.

12

The Coadjutor

JAMES FREDERICK WOOD began life as a Unitarian. He was born in Philadelphia in 1813, and was thus two years younger than John Neumann. His family was English, and young Wood was sent by his parents to school in England when he was a boy. About the time he returned to the United States, his family moved to Cincinnati, and it was here that James Wood embarked upon a career in banking. As a young teller in the bank he made the acquaintance of Cincinnati's bishop, John B. Purcell, and he was much impressed by Bishop Purcell's able and spirited defense of the Catholic Church in a debate with a leading Protestant minister, Alexander Campbell.

In 1835 this debate gained considerable notoriety in the region around Cincinnati, and was the cause of a great many conversions to the Catholic Church, among them James Wood himself. He asked Bishop

Purcell to receive him into the Church and was baptized in May 1836 at the age of twenty-three. About one year later he resigned from the bank and asked Bishop Purcell's permission to study for the priesthood. Realizing Wood's quality, Bishop Purcell sent him to Rome for his seminary training. Seven years later, in 1844, James Wood was ordained by Cardinal Franzoni, and he returned to the United States as a priest of the Diocese of Cincinnati.

His intelligence and urbanity won him early distinction, and by 1848 he was being mentioned seriously as a future bishop. In 1857 he was actually chosen to become the first Bishop of Fort Wayne, Indiana, but at the last minute a change was made and he was appointed instead Coadjutor Bishop of Philadelphia with the right of succession. This meant that he would automatically become the next Bishop of Philadelphia whenever Bishop Neumann died or withdrew from the see for any reason.

James Wood was tall, distinguished in appearance, trained in Rome, a good speaker, witty, urbane and experienced in financial affairs. If the Birthplace of American Independence were to have a coadjutor bishop, Bishop Wood seemed altogether to be a happy choice. Those who thought that Bishop Neumann was perhaps lacking in some of the qualities a bishop ought to have, could find them all in Bishop Wood. Many rejoiced at his appointment but none rejoiced more than Bishop Neumann himself. In his humility the Bishop of Philadelphia welcomed the assistance of an able and zealous coadjutor who

Bishop James Frederick Wood

would help him to administer the affairs of his vast diocese.

The consecration of the new bishop was set for April 26, 1857 in the Cathedral of Cincinnati. Together with three of his priests Bishop Neumann made the journey from Philadelphia to act as co-consecrator with Bishop Purcell and Bishop Richard Whelan of Wheeling, West Virginia. Bishop Wood's mother was still living, and observed the ceremonies from a special place in the sacristy she had chosen for herself.

Also consecrated on the same day was Father Henry Juncker, who had been named the new Bishop of Alton, Illinois. Although Bishop Neumann was not one of the co-consecrators in this ceremony, he was asked to address a reception later in the day given by the Germans of Cincinnati in honor of Bishop Juncker. In his speech Bishop Neumann gave expression to some of his feelings about the role of a bishop in the United States:

> You have scarcely any idea how difficult and painful the office of bishop is, especially here in America. Catholics come from all parts of the world, all nationalities mingle with one another and the bishop is supposed to please all—an impossible task. Where are we to gain strength? Where will Bishop Juncker receive the strength he needs? From the Blood of Christ, from...the Chalice.

Following the consecration, Bishop Neumann and Bishop Wood set out together for Philadelphia. On the way they stopped at the new Redemptorist seminary in Cumberland, Maryland, where Bishop

Neumann conferred Minor Orders on twenty seminarians, and the Subdiaconate on seven more. After leaving Cumberland, they proceeded to Baltimore to attend another consecration, that of Father William Elder, who had been appointed Bishop of Natchez, Mississippi. Father Elder had been a prominent member of the faculty of Mt. St. Vincent's Seminary in Emmitsburg, Maryland, and had been several times mentioned as a candidate for bishop. A few years later, at the close of the Civil War, he would be sent to prison for three months by a Union general for declining to have public prayers said in the Catholic churches of Mississippi for President Abraham Lincoln following his assassination.

Bishop Wood was given a genuinely warm reception when the two bishops finally arrived in Philadelphia, but there was little time for partying. On his very first Sunday in the city he administered Confirmation to a class of children and then went on to preach in three different churches. Work in the city was the program John Neumann had planned for his coadjutor. Bishop Wood would take care of Confirmations and parish visitations in Philadelphia, and would handle routine affairs somewhat like the chancellor of a diocese does today. In addition he would have one other very important assignment: he would be in charge of all the financial affairs of the diocese. Bishop Neumann himself would continue visiting the more remote country districts. This was a work arduous in the extreme, but one which he loved and one which he felt himself especially qualified to perform.

The two bishops lived at first in Bishop Neumann's residence in Logan Square next door to the unfinished Cathedral. The accommodations were hardly palatial. Bishop Neumann was accustomed to live so poorly that there was not enough furniture to go around. When the housekeeper protested that there was no clothes closet for Bishop Wood's room and no money to buy one, Bishop Neumann told her to take his for Bishop Wood since he could get along without one.

Barely two months after he arrived in Philadelphia, Bishop Wood's financial abilities were put to the test. This was the era of railroad building in the United States and as the iron tracks crisscrossed throughout the country, there were fortunes to be made by men who could put themselves in the right place at the right time.

A group of gentlemen in Ohio formed the Ohio Life Insurance and Trust Company and began speculating merrily in railroads. In August 1857 their bubble burst and started a chain reaction which caused a severe depression throughout much of the country. Railroads failed, banks closed and thousands found themselves out of work. That there was considerable chicanery involved in the dealings of the Ohio Life Insurance and Trust Company no one seriously doubted. Bishop Wood himself said in a letter to Bishop Purcell, "It is a pity and a shame that such barefaced and wholesale swindling should go unpunished."

Pennsylvania suffered along with the rest of the country and at one point one-half the workers of

Philadelphia were without jobs. When the state legislature told the Pennsylvania banks not to permit cash withdrawals by their depositors, ten thousand angry men gathered in Independence Square to protest the action.

With so many men out of work, contributions to the Church naturally took a sharp drop, but the action of the legislature actually helped the finances of the diocese. It was the custom of the time for many Catholics to put their money in the keeping of the bishop, thus in effect making him their banker. The bishop could use the money for diocesan purposes, but naturally had to be prepared to pay back the deposits on demand. Had there been a rush by depositors to claim their money, the diocese would have been put in a severe financial crisis, but with the state banks not functioning, most people felt their money was probably safer with the bishop than with anyone else. Therefore a panic was averted, at least as far as the Church was concerned.

In dealing with this crisis and with the other financial affairs of the diocese, Bishop Wood displayed wisdom and prudence, yet we cannot say that he made any radical changes in Bishop Neumann's policies. Even in the matter of finishing the Cathedral, once he had examined the situation, Bishop Wood proceeded slowly, so slowly indeed that some of the outspoken critics of Bishop Neumann now turned their criticism on him.

John Neumann may not have been naturally gifted in financial affairs, but seeing the world with the clear eye of a saint, he put first things first and concentrated on the spiritual needs of his people, trusting in the Providence of God to provide the material means he required. When he saw that new churches, schools and other institutions were needed for his growing flock, he built them, but never did he embark on any outlandish or hare-brained projects. Though the debts were enormous, at no time was the Diocese of Philadelphia seriously in danger of bankruptcy. Ironically, it was Bishop Wood's own former Diocese of Cincinnati which went through a period of financial disaster, though this happened some years after he had left it.

In spite of the fact that John Neumann and James Wood were of very different personalities and temperaments, they got along quite well during the two years and eight months they worked together. Bishop Neumann was genuinely happy to have the assistance of Bishop Wood and trusted him completely. There was, however, a source of disagreement between the two bishops, and it was due to a misunderstanding. We have seen that in 1855, at the Eighth Provincial Council of Baltimore, Bishop Neumann had offered to withdraw from the See of Philadelphia and accept a smaller diocese, even a missionary one, but that he had no time said that he wished to withdraw from the episcopate altogether.

Nevertheless, amid the circulation of rumors and counter-rumors, it seems that Bishop Wood arrived in Philadelphia with the idea that as soon as he was settled as coadjutor, Bishop Neumann intended to resign and turn the diocese over to him. When he discovered that this was not so, he was understandably disappointed and communicated his feelings to Bishop Purcell and his other friends. Some of these men had believed the same rumor, namely that Bishop Wood would indeed become the Bishop of Philadelphia. When they in turn discovered that Bishop Neumann did not intend to resign, they began suggesting that Bishop Wood's talents might be better employed if he were made bishop of another diocese on his own. Even though Bishop Wood's appointment as coadjutor included the right of succession to the See of Philadelphia, both he and Bishop Neumann were, after all, still in their forties, and it might very well be many years before any succession took place.

John Neumann was at first completely unaware of any dissatisfaction on the part of Bishop Wood. When he finally discovered it, he was acutely embarrassed, not for himself but for his coadjutor. With his clear intuition he sensed how keenly disappointed Bishop Wood was at not having been appointed Bishop of Philadelphia in his own right, and he determined to act again at the next provincial council of Baltimore, to be held in May 1858. There, before Archbishop Kenrick and most of the same bishops whom he had addressed three years previously, John Neumann again urged that the Diocese of Philadelphia be divided, and that he be given the new, smaller section. It was apparent by this time that Pottsville would not be suitable as the seat of a new diocese, but Bishop Neumann suggested Easton in the

northeastern part of Pennsylvania. Persuaded by
Neumann's arguments, the other bishops concurred,
and though he did not personally favor the decision,
Archbishop Kenrick forwarded it to Rome.

By this time, of course, Pope Pius IX and his cardinals were well aware of the humility and holiness of
the Bishop of Philadelphia, and they were not much
moved by the rumors, or his own protestations, of
imcompetence. The answer came back from Rome in
November 1858. John Neumann was to remain as
Bishop of Philadelphia with Bishop Wood as his coadjutor, and no decision was to be made about
dividing the diocese until all the bishops of the United
States met in the next plenary council, tentatively
scheduled for 1862. Because of the Civil War, the
Second Plenary Council of Baltimore could not be
held until 1866, and by that time Divine Providence
had intervened to settle the problem of who should be
Bishop of Philadelphia.

Though still disappointed, Bishop Wood accepted
the decision of the Holy See with good grace and a
certain amount of humor. He was given some good
advice in this regard by his friend, Bishop Martin
John Spaulding of Louisville, Kentucky, and he
quoted the advice in a letter to Bishop Purcell,
imitating Bishop Spaulding's Irish brogue: "We are
getting along pretty much as usual. I am trying the
advice of Bishop Spaulding: 'Be *aisy*, and if you can't
be *aisy*, be as *aisy* as you can.'"

Another topic discussed by the bishops at the same
provincial council of Baltimore in 1858 was the

Philadelphia: an early view of the completed Cathedral of Sts. Peter and Paul

question which was tearing the country apart: slavery. Though the bishops in Baltimore, and indeed all the bishops of the country, were under pressure from both sides to take an official stand, they refused to do so. If this decision seems callous to our generation, accustomed as we are to social protests, sometimes even led by the clergy, we must remember that the moral issue of slavery was by this time hopelessly submerged under political and economic interests. The real callousness lay with the politicians and industrialists who made use of the slavery question to further their own selfish ends. Had the bishops issued a public statement, they almost certainly would have been playing into the hands of these unscrupulous men.

The Church has never countenanced the enslavement of one human being by another, either in first-century Rome or in nineteenth-century America, but at neither time was she in a position to make her protest effective. The bishops in America did everything in their power to prevent the outbreak of the Civil War. When all peace efforts failed, they sent priests as chaplains and nuns as nurses onto the very battlefields of the war, and when the fighting ended, they worked tirelessly to help unite a divided and ravished country, and to minister to the spiritual needs of both black and white Americans.

As 1858 faded into 1859, only God knew that this was to be John Neumann's last full year of life. He himself, however, never faltered in the round of labors he had undertaken. He took a special interest in the young seminarians of the diocese and, until his death, insisted on performing all ordinations himself. Now that he had a coadjutor to help him administer the affairs of the city, the schedule he set for himself was, if anything, even more demanding than before. Though Bishop Wood did much of the preliminary work on a variety of matters, the final decision, even in financial affairs, was always Bishop Neumann's.

Bishop Wood, once the question had been definitely settled by Rome, accepted his role of second-in-command without complaint, and performed outstanding services for the Diocese of Philadelphia. If he seemed at times overly critical of his superior, we must not judge him too harshly. Certainly Bishop Neumann never did. The two men differed in nationality, background, character and temperament, and so it not surprising to find a certain abrasion of personality between them. Even the saints sometimes rub each other the wrong way—witness the famous feud between St. Augustine and St. Jerome which lasted for years.

It must be embarrassing, even in heaven, to realize that during your lifetime you were at odds with a saint. Bishop Wood, however, did come to admire John Neumann and to reverence his sanctity. Some years later, now ruler of the diocese and the first Archbishop of Philadelphia, James Wood wrote of his predecessor:

> I had less than three years to enjoy his society, yet long enough to be edified by his example and aided by his advice. I became convinced that he

had all the learning and virtue necessary to adorn the high position which he occupied. I still admire his lively faith, his firm hope, and his burning charity, his fortitude and his constancy in the discharge of all his apostolic duties.

Using the new railroads whenever he could, Bishop Neumann continued to visit the remote parts of his diocese, establishing new parishes and schools, bringing Confirmation to isolated hamlets and even scattered families, saying Mass if necessary in schools and private homes. His last educational project was the establishment of a preparatory seminary in Glen Riddle, Aston, Pennsylvania, not far from Philadelphia. The property is now the motherhouse of the Sisters of the Third Order of St. Francis, the community Bishop Neumann founded in 1855.

In the spirit of his own Order, John Neumann continued to encourage parish missions throughout the diocese. He had the great joy at this time, in a mission preached by the Redemptorists in his own Cathedral parish, of seeing twenty-seven hundred people receive Holy Communion and twenty-three converts admitted to the Church.

The Sisters of the Good Shepherd formed a community of Magdalens during this period, and the Immaculate Heart Sisters from Monroe, Michigan, together with their foundress, Mother Theresa Maxis, began work in the diocese. Through an unfortunate series of misunderstandings between Mother Theresa and Bishop Lefevre of Detroit, the entrance of the Immaculate Heart Sisters into the Diocese of Philadelphia was a stormy one. Bishop Neumann did the best he could to smooth things over, but died before a final settlement was reached. Eventually Mother Theresa was excluded for eighteen years from the Order she had founded, and did not return to it until 1885, seven years before her death. Her community continued to grow, however, and the Immaculate Heart Sisters now form one of the largest teaching Orders in the Archdiocese of Philadelphia.

1859 also saw the completion of one project and the partial completion of another which were dear to Bishop Neumann's heart, and for which he had had to endure much criticism. It almost seemed as though he was being permitted to put his major affairs in order before departing. The orphanage for German-speaking children, upon which the critics had expended so much worry, was finally finished, and the diocese was *not* driven into bankruptcy as had been predicted. Also the new Cathedral began to take shape. The roof was completed and the dome received its copper sheathing by the end of the summer. On the Feast of the Exaltation of the Holy Cross, September 14, an eleven-foot wooden cross covered with gold was raised to the top of the dome in the presence of almost ten thousand people. Though much work remained to be done on the interior of the Cathedral, Bishop Neumann could at last rejoice that the project he had inherited from his predecessor had now become an imposing edifice for all the people of Philadelphia to see.

Christmas passed and the New Year 1860 began.

Bishop Neumann continued his work without pause. He was not feeling well, and cancelled a trip he had planned to Reading, Pennsylvania, but he showed no signs of serious illness—not, that is, until that fateful Thursday afternoon, the fifth of January, when in a few moments all was consummated.

The servant rendered his account and returned to his Master the talents he had gained. In reply he heard the judgment, "Well done, good and faithful servant. Enter into the joy of your Lord."

13

A Father to His People

ALL THE BIOGRAPHIES OF JOHN NEUMANN, including this one, emphasize the fact that he was an ordinary priest and bishop performing the ordinary duties of his office. All of us are called upon to perform the duties proper to our state in life, but you do not become a saint by doing your ordinary duties in just an ordinary way. John Neumann is a saint because he loved and served his Lord, not in an ordinary, but in an extraordinary way. There are commandments, and there are counsels, and the saints follow the counsels of perfection as zealously as the rest of us follow, or should follow, the commandments. To borrow a military phrase, the saints serve and love God above and beyond the call of duty. They are, so to speak, the Church's Medal-of-Honor winners.

St. John Neumann's special relevance to us in America is that he is ours, he was one of us. He traveled through our forests and along our rivers. He walked the streets of our villages and our cities. He labored in places which are familiar to us and said Mass in churches we can still visit. The immigrants for whom he spent himself could have been our ancestors. He helped lay the foundations of the Church in America, our Church, and he inspired a system of schools unique in the world, a system in which many of us received our first education.

St. John Neumann was a man of flesh and blood, like the rest of us. He was not born a saint; he worked hard to become one. To recount his life is to speak of ceaseless activity—after all he took a vow never deliberately to waste a moment of time. But he also led another life—an interior life of prayer and awareness of the presence of God. John Neumann's external activities were performed, not for their own sake, but for the glory of God and the salvation of souls, his own and those which God had placed in his charge. *Soli Deo*, "for God alone," was one of his favorite expressions.

Mother St. John Fournier, Superior of the Sisters of St. Joseph, was one who recognized early what sort of man the Bishop of Philadelphia was:

> His every act, every tone of his voice and manner as witnessed by us in his visitation of our houses and schools bore the unmistakable impress of sanctity. As soon as he entered the house his first visit was to the chapel, where, as he knelt before the altar his whole soul seemed absorbed in God and that air of devout recollection, so habitual to

him, became doubly intensified by his faith in the Sacramental Presence.

Yet he was human like we are. He was wearied by all those labors and travels, and more than once his health was in danger of a complete breakdown. He knew discouragement and frustration, and dryness in his prayers. He experienced temptations against the virtues, and he endured criticism and lack of confidence even from those who should have supported him. He was not endowed with unusual talents or a magnetic personality but he won over his people, both priests and laity, with the earnestness of his manner and the holiness of his life. He was not impressed by the rich or the worldly or the overly-sophisticated, nor did he impress them, but the defect was theirs, not his.

Even as bishop of the largest diocese in the United States, he was always available to any who cared to come looking for him. It was said that no priest in the Diocese of Philadelphia spent as many hours in the confessional as did Bishop Neumann. His room contained only the barest necessities, and he often had but one suit of clothes to his name. Though he tried to conceal it from even his closest associates, he often slept on the bare floor.

He generally arose before five o'clock in the morning, meditated for half an hour, and spent another half hour in the chapel before saying Mass at six. Afterwards he made his thanksgiving while assisting at a second Mass. Then he would hear the confessions of any who were waiting for him, and

VEN. BISHOP JOHN N. NEUMANN
FOURTH BISHOP OF PHILADELPHIA

Chalice and paten used by St. John Neumann

only when these were finished did he take a light breakfast, sometimes nothing but a cup of coffee, before beginning the business of the day.

Once a month, when not away on visitations, he walked across town to spend a day of recollection with his Redemptorist brothers at St. Peter's Church. Not until he died did it become known that he had worn for many years a *cilicium*, or belt of iron wire under this clothes to mortify his flesh.

John Neumann had had to study hard when he was a young man, but he made himself master of theology, philosophy, Canon Law and the other sciences which were necessary for his ministry. Though not endowed with great eloquence, he also labored to become an effective speaker, and his sermons were so obviously sincere and full of unction, that there were few who were not moved. He studied and followed the advice given by holy bishops who had preceded him, men like St. Francis de Sales and St. Alphonsus de Liguori. The words of St. Alphonsus might almost be said to have been written for Bishop Neumann himself, so closely did he follow them: "I recommend to you also not to spare yourself in preaching in all the places of your diocese. The voice of the bishop reaps harvests far more abundant than those of other preachers."

Looking back, who can doubt that God answered, and answered abundantly, the prayer that John Neumann had written just before his ordination in 1836:

Enlighten me, O Sanctifier, that I may present Your Holy Word in truth. Give to my words unction and strength that I may preach them with benefit. With Your Holy Grace grant that Your Word may fall upon good ground from my unworthy lips, and for Your honor bring forth fruit a thousandfold.

We have seen that a few priests were critical of John Neumann as their bishop, but the overwhelming majority venerated him as a true father. He was a firm ruler, but always gentle, and his house was never closed to any priest who wished to see him. When the Know-Nothing Legislature began meddling with church property in 1855, it became necessary that the financial records of each parish be scrupulously kept, and therefore a few negligent priests experienced the bishop's anger, but even John Neumann's disapproval was always tempered with charity and mercy.

To the religious orders of men and women already working in the diocese Bishop Neumann added at least eight more, and provided constant encouragement and support for any who were in need. Mother St. John, whom we have already quoted, had something to say on this point also:

Remarkable was the tenderness of his fatherly solicitude for the religious communities under his care. Their business he made his own and he condescended to enter into the minutest details, where he thought his advice would be of any assistance. Again and again in his letters, he begged them not to hesitate to have recourse to him in every diffi-

Philadelphia: Chestnut Street, about 1856

culty saying, "Whenever you need anything, I beg
you to let me know; if possible I will endeavor to
procure it. . . .I know that God will not forget us."

To a young woman with last-minute doubts about
her religious vocation, the bishop gave the following
advice: "If the day is appointed for your entrance into
religion, do not put it off. If the devil can succeed in
retaining you in the world even for one day, he will
be content because then he may induce you to
abandon your vocation altogether and thus endanger
your eternal salvation."

Besides the churches and schools he built, we have
already mentioned a few of the means Bishop
Neumann used to encourage the devotion and piety
of his people: the Forty Hours' Devotion, so
important in promoting love of Jesus in the Blessed
Sacrament; the confraternities and societies in honor
of our Blessed Lady and the saints; and the parish
missions which brought so many converts into the
Church and so many Catholics back to the practice of
their Faith. Bishop Neumann also encouraged the
exact performance of the Church's liturgy and
published in the United States the first known
Kyriale, or collection of the common chants of the
Mass. He brought a special goldsmith from Baltimore
to care for and repair the sacred vessels, and it is said
that he had a hand in designing the metal case still
used by priests in carrying the holy oils on sick calls.

It was in visiting the outlying districts of his huge
diocese, however, and in bringing his people the
sacrament of Confirmation, which at the time could

be administered only by a bishop, that St. John Neumann showed his remarkable zeal. No village was too remote, no farmhouse too isolated for him to visit. He once spent a whole day riding twenty-five miles through rugged mountain territory to confirm a single child. On these visitations John Neumann made use of any conveyance or any horse, no matter how dilapidated or how sway-backed, which happened to be at hand. More than one traveler in the Pennsylvania mountains at this time, if he had known what to look for, might have seen the bishop of the largest diocese in America riding on the back end of some ancient farm wagon with his feet almost dragging on the ground.

Though he was never given to boisterous laughter, some of these travels provided John Neumann with a chance to display his quiet sense of humor. On one occasion he was being driven by a priest in a borrowed wagon over a rough stretch of road. Crossing a narrow bridge they collided with a larger wagon coming in the opposite direction and broke their wagon-tree, which made it impossible for the horses to continue pulling. Undaunted, the bishop and the priest hitched the horses to the rear, and pulled the wagon themselves to the next farm, where they borrowed some rope and made temporary repairs on their wagon-tree. As they neared the end of their journey, the priest began to let the horses move along a little faster. "Be careful, Father," Bishop Neumann said. "If we break down again, I won't pull any more."

On another occasion, in visiting a convent of sisters, Bishop Neumann found them to be in extreme poverty. "We find it very hard to get along, My Lord," said one of the sisters. "Sometimes we have nothing to make a fire with and then again when we have a fire we have nothing to cook on it." Pointing to a picture of the Crucifixion which hung on the wall, the bishop replied, "There is a book, my sisters, which you must study and meditate on; that sight will make your trials easier, your crosses lighter." Then reaching into his pocket where he was accustomed to keep the religious medals he always distributed on his visits, the bishop said with a twinkle in his eye, "Now I am going to give you some Yankee medals," and handed the Mother Superior fifty dollars in gold pieces.

Though he preferred talking to the poor rather than to the wealthy, and to the simple people rather than to the sophisticated, throughout his priestly life St. John Neumann's great love was to be with the children of any class. From his earliest years as a priest in the area around Buffalo, his pockets had never failed to produce candy and trinkets to reward the scholars who had learned their catechism lessons, and he continued the practice as a bishop. He brought a supply of colored eggs to reward his altar boys after Mass on Easter Sunday, and there were dozens of children in Philadelphia whose first exposure to the wonders of biology was through the bishop's microscope.

One famous story tells of two little girls who visited

Philadelphia: St. Peter's Redemptorist Church
[as it looked in Bishop Neumann's time]

Bishop Neumann one day with a message from the sisters of their school. When the bishop entered the parlor, he found them in wide-eyed admiration of a marble statue of the Infant Jesus lying in a cradle. With a smile he told them that he would give the statue to the one who could carry it home. Being too small to carry the statue very far, the two children were disappointed, but one of them, Margaret McSheffery, returned a short time later with a little wagon to haul her prize away. The sisters at the school were horrified, but Bishop Neumann declared himself bested in the encounter and told Margaret to keep the statue. Later she became Mother General of the Holy Cross Sisters, and the statue remained a prized possession of the motherhouse in Notre Dame, Indiana.

If we may be permitted to quote Mother St. John once more, here is her appraisal of St. John Neumann's love for children:

Of him as of his Divine Master, it might be said that he desired little children to come to him, and when in the midst of the children of the schools or the orphan asylums, he seemed to merge the character of bishop with that of father. He never visited them without bringing games, books, apparatus or such like gifts, thus showing that his heart was indeed all love and kindness. Frequently he might be seen surrounded by a group of children, analyzing a flower or explaining a scientific wonder, adapting his words to their childish comprehension, mingling with his entertainment words of piety and instruction leading them from the contemplation of the beauties of nature to the love of nature's God. Their questions never wearied, their importunities never displeased him.

I remember that on one occasion he was taking a child from St. Vincent's Home, Philadelphia, to an orphan asylum at a considerable distance. He was traveling alone and during the whole journey the poor child (only three years old) was sick, but the good bishop did not think it beneath him to attend to all her wants, and no mother could have been more thoughtful or attentive; he so won the disconsolate little creature's heart that she ever regarded him as her father and wished to make him such in the eyes of others, always speaking of him as *my priest.*

Only God knows how many other souls in the Diocese of Philadelphia thought of St. John Neumann in the same way.

14

Glory

As the news of Bishop Neumann's sudden death spread through the city and the diocese on that fifth of January 1860, some did not at first believe it. When it was confirmed, many wept openly, knowing that they had lost a father and a friend. We can perhaps gain some realization of how people reacted when we recall the effect on the country of another event which happened only a few years ago: President Kennedy's assassination on November 22, 1963.

John Neumann's body, dressed in the purple robes of his office, was first laid in state in his home in Logan Square. After the Masses on Sunday, it was moved next door to the temporary chapel which had been constructed pending the completion of the Cathedral. Father Edward Sourin, the priest who had officially welcomed John Neumann to Philadelphia, now delivered a final eulogy. "He has labored

through every part of the diocese, and has, un-
doubtedly, done more for its better organization and
for the spread of piety throughout the various congregations than might have been otherwise done in even
ten or twenty years by another individual.... He
spared himself in nothing...."

At first it was planned to bury the bishop in the
graveyard of St. John's Pro-Cathedral, but Father
John De Dycker, the Redemptorist Provincial, asked
that he should be buried in the Redemptorist church
of St. Peter's. Bishop Wood left the decision up to
Archbishop Kenrick, and in acceding to the request,
the archbishop said, "Gladly I'll consent to Bishop
Neumann's finding a resting place in death where he
could not find it in life," referring to the fact that John
Neumann had begged to remain a simple Redemptorist and not be compelled to assume the office of
bishop.

On Monday morning, January 9, Bishop Neumann's body was taken from Logan Square, first to
St. John's Pro-Cathedral for the funeral Mass, then
across town to St. Peter's for burial. It was accompanied by the largest funeral procession ever seen in
the history of Philadelphia. All his life John Neumann
had sought to avoid crowds and acclaim, but his
people were determined that he should have them
now. Archbishop Kenrick delivered a moving funeral
oration in which he summarized Bishop Neumann's
achievements, and Father William O'Hara, President
of St. Charles' Seminary, in a letter to Rome,
said:"The Church in America has suffered a great
loss."

Tomb of St. John Neumann
St. Peter's Church, Philadelphia

That loss was not to be permanent, however. Almost as soon as John Neumann was buried in the basement chapel of St. Peter's, people began visiting his tomb, and soon there were stories of marvelous cures gained through his intercession. A woman crippled with open sores on her feet walked away comletely healed, and a child who had never stood before did the same. Hearing was given to the deaf, sight to the blind and peace to those troubled in soul.

In 1886, under Bishop Wood's successor, Archbishop Patrick J. Ryan, the preliminary steps were begun in the examination of John Neumann's sanctity. His cause was officially introduced in Rome in 1897, the first time this had been done for anyone from the United States. Mother Seton would be canonized before John Neumann, but her cause was not officially introduced in Rome until after his.

On December 11, 1921 Pope Benedict xv declared John Neumann's virtues to have been heroic, and ordered that his cause should proceed. Commenting on his virtues, the Holy Father said:

Perhaps the very simplicity of these virtues has been misunderstood by those who thought there was no heroic degree in the virtues of the Servant of God, because in their eyes the good works and holy deeds performed by Neumann are the holy and good deeds which every good religious, every zealous missionary, every good bishop should perform. We shall not pause to remark that works even the most simple, performed with constant perfection in the midst of inevitable difficulties, spell heroism in any servant of God. Just because of the simplicity of his works We find in them a strong argument for saying to the faithful of whatever age, sex or condition: You are all bound to imitate the Venerable Neumann.

In proposing a candidate for beatification, or the right to be called *Blessed*, the Church requires that two miracles be attested and proved. After beatification two more miracles must be approved before the candidate is canonized, or declared a *Saint*. These miracles are generally cures, of disease or injuries, granted by God to individuals through the intercession of the candidate in question. The cures are subjected to a most rigorous and painstaking examination, and in order to be declared miraculous, they must be shown to be absolutely beyond the power of medical science either to effect or to explain.

In the cause of John Neumann, the first miracle proved was that of Eva Benassi, an eleven-year-old girl living in the town of Sassuolo, Italy. She was a student at the Institute of St. Joseph, conducted by the Sisters of the Third Order of St. Francis. In May 1923, while at school, Eva complained of a headache, abdominal pain and fever. No ordinary remedies were of any help and by the third day the physicians diagnosed her illness as acute diffused peritonitis. On the fifth day Eva received the Last Sacraments of the Church, and the doctor informed her father and the sisters that death was imminent and could be expected perhaps during the night.

One of the nuns, Sister Elizabeth Romoli, who had a devotion to Bishop Neumann, began praying to him, and between eight and nine o'clock in the evening she placed a picture of Bishop Neumann on Eva's stomach. During the night Eva awoke and told Sister Elizabeth that she no longer felt the pain, the nausea or the fever she had experienced before. By morning her symptoms had disappeared completely, and she seemed to be entirely cured. She was able to leave the hospital and to resume her studies at school.

During the consideration of the cure, Eva Benassi was examined again in December 1960. She was then forty-eight years old and the mother of two grown children. She was in perfect health and showed no signs of any peritonitis.

The second of John Neumann's miracles approved by the Church occurred near Philadelphia in July 1949. James Kent Lenahan, aged nineteen, was riding in an automobile with two of his friends in Villanova, a suburb of Philadelphia. As he stepped out of the car near his home, the driver lurched ahead and Lenahan was left clinging to the side and top of the automobile. The car then sideswiped a utility pole, crushing Lenahan and throwing him to the ground. When he was admitted to Bryn Mawr Hospital, his skull was crushed, one eye torn from its socket, his lung was pierced, three ribs and his collarbone broken, and he had other internal complications. His condition was considered to be so bad that the hospital did not even attempt to detail all his injuries. His temperature rose to 107° and his pulse to 160. All hope for his recovery was abandoned.

His parents, however, brought a piece of Bishop Neumann's cassock which they had obtained, and placed it upon young Lenahan in the hospital. By 11:00 P.M. the same day his temperature had dropped to 100° and his pulse was almost normal. This was July 12, four days after the accident. By July 17 his temperature and pulse were completely normal and he was on the way to full recovery. On August 10 he was released from the hospital.

His mother testified later: "He was out mowing the front lawn in a couple of weeks and by Labor Day he was back playing his trumpet and lifting weights." He is now married and the father of a family. He has had no serious illness since his accident in 1949.

In February 1963 the Holy See approved both these cures as miraculous, and June 23 was fixed for John Neumann's beatification. Pope John xxiii died that June, however, and so the ceremony was postponed. John Neumann was finally beatified by Pope Paul vi on October 13, 1963 in St. Peter's Basilica.

A year previously, in October 1962, another young Philadelphia boy, Michael Flanigan, began having trouble with his leg. After several unsuccessful operations, his affliction was diagnosed as cancer of the bone which had spread also to the lungs. Since his case seemed hopeless, he was discharged from the hospital and sent home. He was given six months to live.

In July 1963 Michael's parents began taking him to Bishop Neumann's shrine at St. Peter's Church in Philadelphia. Almost immediately his appetite improved and he began to put on weight. By October there was no longer a tumor in his left lung and by

Rome: Beatification ceremony of John Neumann
St. Peter's Basilica, October 13, 1963

December 1963 his right lung was also clear. The bone cancer in his leg had disappeared as well. Since that time Michael has enjoyed good health, and has had no recurrence of the cancer.

After accepting this cure as an authentic miracle, Pope Paul acted as he had done in the case of Mother Seton, and dispensed John Neumann's cause from the requirement of a second miracle. The canonization was set for June 19, 1977, to be held, like Mother Seton's, outside in St. Peter's Square.

Though other American bishops have been mentioned as possible candidates for canonization, John Nepomucene Neumann is the first of the American hierarchy ever to be raised to the altars of the Church. His feast day is celebrated on the anniversary of his death, January 5.

Thus the humble country boy from Bohemia has become one of the glories of the Church in the United States. He who never sought worldly honors has gained the greatest honor any mortal can attain: to be proclaimed a saint by the Vicar of Christ. John Neumann's life was three months short of forty-nine years, but he fulfilled much in that brief span.

As he looks down from the high place he holds in heaven, we are confident that he will join with St. Frances Xavier Cabrini and St. Elizabeth Seton in interceding for, and in protecting his adopted country. He lived among us and worked in our midst. We pray that he will help us, as he helped so many of our ancestors, to grow in the knowledge and love of God, and to walk in the way of eternal salvation.

PICTURE CREDITS